A
View
FROM THE
Porch

A
View
FROM THE
Porch

Overcoming Our Giants

by
DEB WEISEN

XULON PRESS

Xulon Press
2301 Lucien Way #415
Maitland, FL 32751
407.339.4217
www.xulonpress.com

Printed in the United States of America

Paperback ISBN-13: 978-1-6628-1770-0
Ebook ISBN-13: 978-1-6628-1771-7

TABLE OF CONTENTS

PREFACE

I have had the privilege of being in Christian ministry for over forty-four years, including twenty-five years as a children's and family life director. For the past ten years, I have served as an ordained minister in an associate pastor role.

Throughout my ministry, I have witnessed many dedicated believers—some of whom seemed caught in perpetual struggle from one crisis to the next, while others seemed to thrive in the face of adversity. After much thought, prayer, and study, coupled with a deep empathy for those who suffer, God has revealed some life-changing insights into overcoming the giants in our lives. There are essential choices people make that either hinder their spiritual journey or enable them to walk confidently in faith despite difficult circumstances.

All of us face difficult circumstances in our life journeys. Why do some people seem to receive more than their fair share of pain and suffering? Honestly, I have questioned God many times, seeking an answer even in those times when I could not sense His presence or see Him moving on my behalf. Sometimes, God's plan for me remains beyond my finite comprehension, but I have found the use of a few simple principles can give peace and encouragement in the darkest of times. I have come to realize that every day I must choose to *not* trust the giants in my life, but to trust God alone. Giants have a way of causing me to believe that they are more powerful than God Almighty. This is a smoke-and-mirrors illusion the enemy frequently uses, and we must be on guard constantly to not lose sight of who is fighting our battles.

Recently, a few of my friends were having a conversation. One shared that her husband and son love to restore cars. She described the process of restoration as hard work that takes time, perseverance, and commitment. Another friend mentioned that often the parts used in the restoration as replacements are stronger than the originals.

Wow! What a great metaphor to keep in mind as we consider the principles in the following chapters to help us thrive in difficult circumstances. The Holy Spirit promises to empower us when we stand firm through each battle and will help us emerge stronger on the other side.

On February 1, 1975, I attended a weekend event called a Lay Witness Mission. The entire focus of the weekend was the teaching that if I would develop a daily quiet time every morning to meet with Jesus to study and pray, I would be able to live a victorious life in Him. By the end of that weekend, I had made the decision to totally commit my life 100 percent to God and commit to meet with Him every day. To this day, I continue to practice this habit of spending time with God daily. I attribute the joy of living my life in faith to this practice. God alone has a creative solution to every problem, and by yielding to Him daily, I remain open to His leading and His encouragement.

Now ... what you will *not* find in this book is a brilliant, intellectual summation of the Christian walk. What you *will* find is an honest, vulnerable, and truthful account of how bowing before God and committing to follow Him can change not only your daily routine, but also your fundamental well-being, and spiritual and emotional health.

As you read this book, I pray *you* discover insights that help you refocus your life and find encouragement. *Never give up w*hen facing your giants. Remember, these formidable obstacles can be broken down when we have the right strategy in place and go into battle armed and prepared.

Chapter 1

A VIEW FROM THE PORCH

*I lift up my eyes to the mountains—where
does my help come from? My help comes from
the Lord, the Maker of heaven and earth.*
Psalm 121:1–2

It was one of those "special" days—a bright, sunny summer
day—when I found myself at wit's end in a battle with
my kids. I realized the only way to achieve peace was to
divide and conquer. I decided it was time for Andi, our
nine-year-old daughter, to have a timeout and Tyler, our
six-year-old son, to have a quiet time of his own on our
front porch.

I sent Andi to her room, knowing full well it was more
a reward than a form of punishment. Andi loved to read,
and readily accepted *any* opportunity to retreat to her

little "hideaway." A natural speed-reader with a near-photographic memory, she would be occupied for an extended period, lost in her favorite book.

I took Tyler outside with me and told him he had to stay on the front porch while I mowed the front lawn. You can imagine how that might go for an active six-year-old little boy stuck on the front porch. Although he was *not* a happy camper, I knew he would not move from that spot until he had permission to do so. You see, God had blessed me with at least one compliant child. With everyone settled in their respective places, I started the lawnmower.

I looked up as I finished the first pass. Tyler had taken up his position on the porch—arms crossed, head down, and pouty lower lip forced out as far as possible—a perfect picture of dejection. I continued to push the mower on another pass, then another. As the rhythm of the motor droned on, I soon found myself reflecting on my role as a mother. It included some rather heavy self-talk with questions like, "*Am* I a good mom?" and "Are my kids going to turn out okay?"

I was deep into my conversation with myself, when suddenly, I felt the grip of a little hand around my arm from behind. Instantly, I knew something was terribly wrong. Tyler was yelling, "Mommy, look!"

He was pointing down the road where our eighty-year-old neighbor, Margaret, was frantically waving her arms and screaming for help. I had not heard her cries above the noise of the mower and the fact that I was absorbed in thought. I quickly grabbed Tyler's hand and we ran down to see what was wrong.

Margaret urgently explained that Breece, her husband, had fallen. He'd had a seizure, and she couldn't get him up off the floor. Every time he had one of these episodes, he needed medication immediately. She had tried to get his medication to him but could not open the container. The nurse had been there earlier and left a new prescription, but had forgotten to transfer the medication from the child-proof bottle into one Margaret could easily open. With her severe arthritis, opening one of those caps was impossible. Somehow, Margaret and I managed to get her husband into a chair, albeit with great difficulty. I quickly helped her with his medication and within just a few minutes things began to settle down and everything returned to normal. Before we left, Tyler helped me transfer the medication into the little bottle for Margaret. Each of us gave hugs all around, and we returned home, happy that we'd been able to help.

I did not know it, but in the next few moments my perspective would change forever. As Tyler and I made our way back up the road to the house, he looked up at me and said, "Mom, God really used us."

"He sure did." I replied.

Then Tyler said something very profound that literally stopped me in my tracks.

"Mom, I'm sure glad I looked up."

I stood there in the middle of the road, still trying to grasp what I'd just heard. I asked him to repeat it.

"Mom! I *said* I'm glad I looked up."

In that moment with Tyler, I realized the truth was so simple: "Look up." When we choose to look up, God gives us a new focus and a new perspective in order that we might see above our circumstances.

There it was—straight from the mouth of a child. How many times in my life had I been on the porch and taken up my position? Countless times, for sure. I would sit there asking, "Why me?" and thinking, "Poor me," and wondering how much longer I would be stuck on the porch; wondering if anyone would understand what I felt and constantly blaming others for my circumstances. Often, I could see nothing but the circumstances that surrounded me. Just look up!

Here's another nugget of truth I received from God that day. Tyler still had a few minutes left on his timeout. I knew after all that drama, and as hard as it was, I needed to be consistent with my discipline. I told Tyler he needed to go back to the porch until I finished mowing the lawn, and then he could go play. With an obedient nod, he headed for the porch. As I returned to the mower, I stole a glance Tyler's way to see how he was taking the remaining time-out. He had once again taken up his position, but this time was different. Instead of focusing on his own dilemma, he had turned his attention outward. There he was on tiptoe, peering expectantly over the porch rail like a kid at a parade watching to see what was coming next. He surveyed the area in every direction on constant watch. I found myself laughing out loud and hoping he was settled in for the long haul. Tyler's entire attitude was refocused on a higher level. He was now looking up *and* expecting something new.

What a difference. Once Tyler took his eyes off his circumstance and looked up, he had a new perspective and was eager to be used again. He was no longer sitting on the porch with arms crossed, feeling sorry for himself and miserable in his circumstance.

How about you? Do you find yourself on the porch, taking up *your* position? Is your focus totally on the porch—the circumstances in your life? Maybe *you* need to look up.

2 Chronicles 20 relates the story of King Jehoshaphat. Life was good, and he had just turned the entire nation of Judah back to God. Then, suddenly vast armies were attacking from all sides and coming to make war against him. Jehoshaphat quickly called the people together to fast and pray. In verse 12 we read, *"O, our God, will you not judge them? For we have no power to face this vast army that is attacking us. We do not know what to do, but our eyes are upon you!"*

Can it be that easy? Doesn't it make sense that living with our eyes focused upward and off ourselves, we can live more expectantly even in difficult circumstances? When it seems that life is caving in all around you, remember the words of King Jehoshaphat and declare, *"Though I am powerless against my circumstances, my eyes are upon You."* If you are stuck on the porch, it's time to refocus and look to Him.

Chapter 2

NEW LIFE OR
HOPELESS DREAMS?

I will praise the Lord no <u>matter what</u>
<u>happens</u>. *I will* constantly speak of his glories
and grace. *I will* boast of all his kindness to
me. Let all who are discouraged *Take Heart*.
                                    Psalm 34:1–8

F or six years, Jeff and I had wanted to start a family.
During that time, we were never without good advice.
We had been encouraged to try "nooners," "afternooners,"
or "crack-of-dawners"—whenever the thermometer dis-
played the appropriate temperature. Whether it was the
doctor, friends, or family, we were eager to accept advice
from anyone. It was quite an adventure for us. We usually
kept a good sense of humor and had a good time trying.

It seemed all our friends had already begun their families—some with two or more children. I was happy for all of them, yet deep down I was beginning to feel desperate for a child of my own. In Genesis 30, Rachel wants to die if she can't have a baby. I read that scripture and realized I was beginning to relate to her discontent and disillusionment.

I fought jealousy and secretly harbored disappointment in God for not blessing us with children. I journaled daily and prayed while repenting and asking for forgiveness for not trusting God's timing. Every morning I would renew my commitment to completely trust Him. Without my daily quiet time, I know I would have become bitter and hopeless.

On the day I finally did find out I was expecting, I called everyone I knew with the news within two hours after we left the doctor's office. Of course, this was a secret I just could *not* keep to myself. And this was *before* social media. We were soon making plans to decorate a nursery. It was exciting and great fun not knowing whether we would have a boy or a girl. It made no difference to us.

Four weeks before the long-awaited day, I woke to find my water had broken. *Surprise!* We quickly called the doctor, who asked, "Are you sure that is what happened?" (You just gotta love this kind of question. How could I possibly miss this one?) I stayed calm and resisted the urge to say, "No, duh." We were given instructions to get right to the hospital.

Upon admission to the maternity ward, the nurses had me begin walking the halls to help start the contractions. Six hours later I was still walking the halls and chatting with people, and *still* no contractions. Finally, my labor pains began that evening. We put our Lamaze training to the test and were quite the team. I kept hyperventilating because

I was not doing my breathing quite right, but with Jeff's instruction and support, I managed to get through with no medication.

However, a few doors down the hall, another woman was screaming with every contraction. We found it rather terrifying and at the same time quite humorous. I'm very competitive, and this gave me the determination to suffer quietly. We *still* laugh about it.

Jared Scott Weisen was born at 11:16 p.m., which happened to be right in the middle of the nursing team shift change. The nurses seemed to enjoy our interaction when it came to my "suffering" and Jeff's "humor." Because of the camaraderie we'd experienced together, we were delighted when they stayed on and both nursing teams watched the delivery and then celebrated the moment with us. However, the celebration was short-lived. Jared was immediately put in an incubator and rushed off to the NICU (Neonatal Intensive Care Unit).

I spent the remainder of that night in restless fits of sleep. The next morning after taking a shower, I made my way down the hall to the intensive care to see my baby boy. Just as I reached the NICU window, I heard the elevator open and out stepped Jeff. It was 6:00 a.m. As we held hands and gazed at our son, the nurse quietly walked over, smiled—a sort of sad smile—and pulled down the blind blocking our view. It was at that moment we realized for the first time that little Jared was in trouble.

We were informed soon after that our son was not doing well. How could that be? He weighed six pounds and looked so healthy next to the other tiny "preemies." The doctor soon came out and told us that our little man needed to stop fighting so hard in order that he might live. What a paradox—stop trying so hard to live, then we can save you—or is it?

How many times in life do we struggle and try everything we know to fix things? Instead, our first choice needs to be turning to God with honesty, throwing our fear, frustration, doubt, and hopelessness right at the feet of Jesus. It is a proven fact that doing the opposite of what is natural is a powerful weapon against fear. Naturally, we isolate and turn ourselves inside out with worry. Supernaturally, we can practice being thankful and trusting that God *is* much bigger than all that we fear. Take this to the bank: When we stop struggling and begin trusting and thanking God, He moves in and brings us to a point of peace.

It was a beautiful Sunday morning, and we knew the family was getting ready for church. As I sensed panic begin to grip me, I felt we would need all the encouragement we could find. We quickly called our family with the news, and they in turn called every prayer warrior in the church. Our next call was to our pastor. He arrived shortly after the morning worship service. Jared's condition slowly worsened with every hour that passed. We asked about having him anointed and dedicated to the Lord. The pastor agreed, and the three of us stood beside Jared's incubator. Although we were unable to hold our son, the pastor laid his hands on him and prayed over him. The dedication of our baby was heartbreaking and yet strangely comforting. We were reminded that as parents we have an awesome responsibility to raise and to teach our children to love and obey God. If that opportunity was not to be, we knew our son was a gift and ultimately belonged to the Father. Nonetheless, it was humbling and extremely painful to give back what we could not keep.

This was not the "normal" baby dedication where friends and family gathered around to support and encourage. At the same time, however, I thought since it was Sunday and everyone would soon know about our situation, God would surely touch Jared, he would be healed, and everything would be just as I planned. Somehow, I had come to feel all my good works would certainly ensure God loved me enough to save my son. I knew that to be false teaching, but in my desperation, I struggled to lean on His grace and mercy. I had a plan and was trying hard to make God small enough to fit into it. Could He not see that this miracle could bring Him glory and honor? Was I bargaining with God?

How could this be happening?

At 6:10 that evening, the doctor walked into my room, and with tears in his eyes, he told us that the battle was over for Jared. Our son was now in the arms of Jesus. I remember clearly looking at Jeff and saying, "I want two things: I want to hold my son, and I want to go home. **Now!**"

Soon after, they brought our son into the room. He was wrapped in a soft baby blanket. With grandparents, aunts, and uncles circling the bed, we held our little guy, unwrapped him and looked at every single part of his body. We kissed each finger and toe. We softly caressed his cheeks, then his nose, even his lips. We found even the smallest details to be perfect in every way. He was beautiful.

We were together in this most serene, tender, and precious moment for nearly an hour. We carefully wrapped Jared up in the blanket as if tucking him into bed and kissed him goodnight. Then I tenderly handed my son to the nurse.

I had never felt so empty...

They immediately brought a wheelchair for me, and we left the hospital with empty hearts and shattered dreams. Family wanted to gather at our house, but Jeff wisely told them to give us a few hours alone. We entered the house and slowly walked down the hall to our beautiful nursery. We fell into each other's arms and literally collapsed on the floor. We grieved deeply in those moments with uncontrolled sobs—the kind that made it hard to catch a breath.

Jeff began to pray. I do not remember every word, but I do remember when he said, "Lord, somehow use this." I fell back from him still in anguish and deep pain and said, "I don't want to be used. I want my baby!" As we knelt on that floor, we both cried from deep within our souls.

Three weeks after Jared's death, we received the news from our doctor that Jared had been overcome by a virus that I had carried. I was stunned. All I heard was, "He died because of you." I was instantly sick, literally. Talk about kicking someone when they were already down.

All I could do was cry out to God for answers. I stopped praying the words I thought He wanted to hear. I prayed *in* my deep anguish and pain. I was completely honest with Him. That is not easy, but I had to come to a place where I could lay it all out in front of God. Being vulnerable is a scary thing. It means trusting God for your reputation, your daily choices, your successes, failures, hopes, and dreams—even when your dreams shatter and God's presence seems so distant.

No words in scripture are more applicable to me than the following from the Living Bible paraphrase. They helped me stand firm then, and they have the very same power today. I refer to these as the "I Wills."

*I **will*** praise the Lord no <u>matter what hap-</u>
<u>pens</u>. *I **will*** constantly speak of his glories
and grace. *I **will*** boast of all his kindness
to me. Let all who are discouraged ***take***
heart. Let us ***praise*** the Lord together and
exalt his name. For I *cried* to him and he
answered me! He **freed me** from all my
fears. Others, too, were **radiant** at what he
did for them. Theirs was no downcast look
of rejection! This poor man cried to the
Lord—and the Lord heard him and saved
him out of his troubles. For the Angel of
the Lord guards and rescues all who rev-
erence him. *Oh, put God to the test and see
how kind he is! See for yourself the way his
mercies shower down on all who trust in him*
(Ps. 34:1–8).

When one surrenders in battle, he shows his intentions
by waving a white flag, raising arms high above his head
while ceasing to resist. Are you at a point in your life when
fighting further seems pointless with no victory in sight?
Do you want to return home to the place where you are
loved and can experience a radiant joy in living? Then surrender your pain and suffering to God and trust Him. He
is faithful and you *can* trust His Word. You *will* find true
freedom in Him.

Surrender and trust are the avenues to find your joy
again. He will enable your smile to emerge from deep within
and allow your eyes to sparkle. When a person is plagued
by grief and bitterness, there is no radiance or sparkle that
attracts others and points them to the Savior. I am confident

that *surrendered* suffering can be a blessing. I know this is not always easy, but I also know without any doubt it *is* possible to find joy again when we turn to Him.

In the days that followed Jared's death, I learned much about staying open and not isolating myself from others. Allowing people to serve and help me encouraged me and blessed them. Even when they offered well-intentioned platitudes like, "Time will heal," or "You'll have another child," I was able to appreciate their presence if not their words of encouragement. I was able to think of times I'd fallen short in offering condolences. At times I had not even approached grieving friends, for fear of saying the wrong thing. These brave people were there for me, so I chose to hear their hearts above their words.

I remember the day my emotional healing began. My sister-in-law, Jennifer, who lived in California, called and asked me what Jared looked like. I began to describe my son in every detail, and as I did, I could feel joy and pride as I knew any mother would. I am so thankful she had the courage to ask me that question.

Slowly, I began to realize that I had to live *in* praise. This means moving on with my life while allowing God to reveal my need for a grateful heart. For example, instead of dwelling on the loss, I began to appreciate the process. Some of my friends never knew the joy of carrying a child and hearing that first cry at birth. I can remember it like it was yesterday. Choosing to delight in this and other memories filled my heart. I thank God for His healing touch and tender mercies.

Each time I made a specific choice to be thankful, I was able to take heart and move forward. The scripture says, *"Let us praise the Lord together!"* Ps. 34:3 I could *not* consistently live *in* a thankful attitude on my own. For instance, when I began to blame myself, Jeff would have no part in it. He refused to let me wallow and try to place any blame on myself. By staying open and turning to God, I was willing to accept my husband's support and persuasion, which allowed me to redirect my thoughts away from feelings and circumstances. Being willing to lean on family and friends was key. With their encouragement, I was able to praise God regardless of my circumstances. It was not easy to be served, but the blessings were amazing.

I took God at His word and put my faith and trust in Him. That enabled me to learn to thrive again, not just survive another day. I still had no child, and my circumstances had not changed, but my outlook became expectant and hopeful. Spending time with Jesus daily created a hope in me that I **would** completely recover. I admit, many days of prayer and study seemed a waste, but perseverance paid off.

Less than one year after this horrible loss, I had my first opportunity to speak at a women's retreat. The theme was "Victor or Victim." I found I had a message to give because I was daily learning to be a victor. I have spoken for over thirty-four years to more than 1,100 groups. Jeff and I have shared our story at couples retreats and marriage weekends. We have seen God use our brokenness to encourage others to stand firm in their faith. Even if they could not relate to our specific loss, they *could* relate to the disappointment and hopelessness we experienced. They could relate to being honest with God and with being vulnerable and allowing others to come alongside them with support. They could connect with the realization that denying pain leads to bitterness and hopelessness. Most importantly, they were reminded that what the enemy means for evil, God will redeem and use for His glory if we allow Him.

Today, choose to walk away from your pain, bitterness, self-pity, and loneliness. With an open heart, walk right into the open arms of Jesus. Why not choose to be freed from all your fears and rejection? As you practice being thankful and honest, you will see God's persistent presence at work in your life. The Holy Spirit will help you persevere and develop permanent life-changing habits, one choice at a time. Through the power of the Spirit, begin to *praise the LORD no matter what happens.*

Chapter 3

LOVE AT FIRST SIGHT

No temptation has seized you except what is common to man. And God is faithful, he will not let you be tempted beyond what you can bear. But when you are tempted, he will also provide a way out so that you may stand up under it.

1 Corinthians 10:13

I *love* to fish. I will fish for anything, anytime. I enjoy the wait and the anticipation of the catch. The day can be long or short—it just doesn't matter because I'm fishing. When someone else has a fish on, I don't sit there and think life isn't fair. I don't quit fishing and feel sorry for myself because no one understands that I can't wait one minute longer. When the "bite" isn't on (so to speak), some want to give up and go home right away. Not me. I sit quietly and think to myself, "My turn is coming. I'll soon get to yell, 'Fish On!'"

Following the loss of our little boy, Jeff and I could easily have said, "*That* was too painful. We cannot survive that heartache again. So, we are done trying to have children."

We could have accepted the thought that life is not fair. However, I do not believe this is the path God has set before us. Settling for something less prevents us from achieving our intended purpose. Vibrant, thriving Christians live each day in expectation of divine assignments direct from the Master Designer Himself.

Thinking back, I remember more than once I felt like God had given me more than I could bear. I memorized the scripture above and used it regularly to help me place my efforts and thoughts back on God and not on my circumstances. This scripture reminds me that God will keep His promises even when things seem impossible.

I was recovering from my loss, but *every* morning I had to commit my day to God's glory, or I would find myself struggling with loss and emptiness. I knew I was making some progress, but doubt and fear always seemed to linger close by, just waiting for me. At times I found myself angry with God. I was ready to move on, but how?

If we wait on God, He *will* provide a way out so we can stand up under it. A couple of months later, some friends suggested we investigate becoming foster parents. We brushed it aside with barely a thought, and before long we had returned to our regular routine. Little did we know we would soon begin another journey that would prove one of the greatest challenges of our lives.

It was 6:00 p.m. and the evening news was on the local television station. I was distracted with preparing dinner and not really paying attention. I happened to glance at the TV and saw an "**Alert**" crossing the screen: "**Foster Parent Program in desperate need of Foster Parents.**" My heart skipped a beat, and I quickly turned to Jeff and said, "Honey, look!" He looked up, rolled his eyes, and said, "Deb, we're not ready for this. After what we've been through, we cannot do this."

"Oh," was all I said.

One month later, we were driving around the block, looking anxiously for a parking spot at the Department of Social and Health Services for the state of Washington. We were running late for our first orientation meeting for foster parents—*not* a great way to make a first impression. We hurried in the door and took two seats near the back of the room, hoping no one noticed us. A lady was introduced as a long-time foster parent, and she began sharing a story about one of her high school-aged foster kids who forced his way through her kitchen door using an axe. *An axe? Are you kidding me?* We looked at each other as if to say, "Did you just hear what I just heard?" Jeff leaned over and loudly whispered, "Why on earth are we here?" I wondered if this was their way of weeding out prospective foster parents who were faint of heart. Was this an isolated incident or was this normal? Why *were* we here?

Thankfully, our heart rates returned to normal during the remainder of the orientation. We heard many more encouraging stories of children's lives affected by the love and compassion of other foster parents. There were stories of people who accepted kids of all ages into their homes, where these children could experience some sense of safety and routine. Several more training sessions followed, along with a home-study. We officially received our stamp of approval and became a foster home for short-term care of preschool- through elementary-age children. A short-term stay was defined as one week to three months. We had kids coming, staying, and going on a regular basis. This proved to be helpful to my healing process, as it gave me something into which I could pour my life. Caring for these children gave me renewed purpose and joy.

One year later, we had lost count of the actual number of foster children we had welcomed into our home. On the morning of Friday, October 10, 1980, we opened the front door to our newest foster child. A small, dark-haired boy stood on our front porch clutching a black-and-white cat like a favorite rag doll. The caseworker gave us the background information and his business card, then turned and left. The first thing we noticed was how quiet and reserved this little guy was. The second was that he looked just like Jeff. We asked his name and, looking at the floor, he quietly said, "Eddie." The cat's name was "Boots," for its four white paws.

The three of us spent the rest of the day getting acquainted while having fun doing various activities. That evening I thought cookies and milk before bedtime would be a great idea. When I retrieved the hot cookies from the oven, I asked Jeff to have Eddie come to the table. Jeff called him, thinking he was just in the other room. He did not respond, and after ten minutes of searching every room upstairs and downstairs, we finally found him under his bed with his cat, pressed against the back corner of the room. It took another ten minutes to coax Eddie and Boots out from under the bed. Oh, what this young boy must have endured.

After cookies and milk, we were sitting in the living room, and I had Eddie cuddled in my arms. Jeff got out his guitar and we began singing children's choruses from Sunday School. We were singing a song titled, "If I Were a Butterfly," by Ernie Rettino & Debbie Kerner Rettino, from *"The Kids' Praise Album"*. The lyrics go something like,

If I were a butterfly, I'd thank you, Lord,
for giving me wings.
And if I were a robin in a tree, I'd thank you, Lord,
that I could sing.
And if I were a fish in the sea,
I'd wiggle my tail, and I'd giggle with glee.
But I'd just thank you, Father, for making me Me. '
Cause you gave me a heart, and you gave me a smile.
You gave me Jesus, and you made me your child.
And I just thank you, Father, for making me Me.
I just thank you, Father, for making me, Me, Me, Me."

We finished that last line of the chorus when, without warning, Eddie burst into tears and sobbed uncontrollably. Nothing we said or did gave any comfort or peace to this little guy, whose heart was obviously tormented. After holding him for what seemed like hours, we were out of ideas. His little body heaved in convulsing sobs, causing him to throw up several times. He could barely breathe. Of course, it was late Friday night, and our caseworker was not available until Monday—like he would be able to help, anyway. We looked at each other as if to say, "Now what?"

Shortly after, the words to a familiar song came to mind. Jeff began playing the song, and I began to sing softly, "Jesus, Jesus, Jesus, there's just something about that name."

Almost immediately, we noticed the sobs were subsiding, and before we'd finished the song, Eddie was slumped in my arms, eyes closed, and appeared to be resting comfortably. I cannot emphasize enough how important it has been to me throughout my life to speak the name of Jesus. His is a beautiful, wonderful, and *powerful* name. That night I witnessed the Spirit of God move in and literally bring peace to one of His precious children.

Little did we know that in his first five years, Eddie had been so wounded physically, mentally, and emotionally that nothing short of a complete miracle would ever free him from his past abuse and neglect. When he first arrived, he was on a regular, heavy dose of Ritalin. We decided to take him off the Ritalin, and that was when the fun began. We experienced firsthand the living definition of ADD and ADHD with a *highly* active and almost desperate little guy who challenged every boundary. He was defiant, angry, and extremely needy. And yet, at times he seemed to respond to our attempts at consistency, structure, and love. Over the next few months, we fell in love with Eddie in spite of everything and hoped one day to make him ours.

On May 1, 1981, Jeff and I adopted Eddie on his sixth birthday. We stood in front of the judge as he told us that when adopting a child, there was no turning back. He asked us if we were sure about taking Eddie as our own. At that moment, we were sure about our decision and we answered, "We accept Eddie as our son." The three of us had become a family. We believed that with God's help, Eddie's deep emotional wounds would soon be healed.

I'm reminded of our first visit as a family to Nampa, Idaho, to see my folks on their farm. Having been a school administrator for years and working with all types of kids on the spectrum, I asked my stepdad what he thought about Eddie. He said, "Eddie will either be the president of the United States or the best criminal we've ever seen." His words would come back to me many times over the following years.

We fell into a routine and together were able to care for Eddie. We quickly realized that every time a new foster child entered our home, within a few days there was total chaos. It was not long before we decided to call DSHS and let them know we could no longer take any foster children. That was not an easy call, because our time as foster parents had been an amazing experience and seen us through a difficult time. However, if we had any hope of helping Eddie heal, we needed to be totally focused on him.

One week after making that decision, just a week before Halloween, we received an urgent call from DSHS, asking if we would consider one more child before we let our license lapse. The caseworker began by saying, "This child will be up for adoption. This child is a two-year-old little girl. She has been with one foster mom since she was one." When I took the call, I was working at our print shop. I was at one end and Jeff was at the other end of our shop. I began waving my arms trying to get his attention. When he came over, I put the caseworker on hold and explained the situation to Jeff. I was talking so fast, he could barely understand me. He just stood looking at me with an odd expression. Then finally, he said, "It has to be a God thing."

When I opened the door the following day, a cute little girl stepped over the threshold, put her hands on her hips, smiled, and said, "Hi, I'm Andi. What's your name?" She was as big around as she was tall. Little rolls of fat on her arms and legs made her absolutely adorable—a chubby little face with two, one-inch pigtails sticking straight out the top of her head. It truly was love at first sight.

I remember the first lunch we all had together as if it were yesterday. I put Andi's sandwich in front of her and with great authority she said, "Uh, 'cuse me, I don't eat dat. I eat dat!" She was pointing to the top of the refrigerator where we kept the potato chips. Jeff and I both laughed, and I said, "You can eat that," pointing to the chips, "when you eat that," pointing to her sandwich. She folded her arms, extended her lower lip, and the battle began.

This little girl was physically abused before she was one year old. She'd had her arm broken, two skull fractures, and a third-degree cigarette burn under one eye. However, because of the love of an incredible foster mom named Maggie, Andi's natural exuberance for life had been nurtured and encouraged.

The next couple months were challenging as the four of us continued to find our way as a family. The dynamics between Andi and Eddie alternated between being genuinely touching and downright scary. However, that's a story for another chapter.

Just eight short weeks after Andi arrived, we were busy getting ready for our first Christmas together. On the day before Christmas Eve, we received a call from DSHS and were told Andi's parents would not relinquish their rights and that we would have to return Andi to her parents the following day. We were shocked and devastated, especially since we'd also been told that both parents would most likely abuse again.

We quickly called family and threw together an early Christmas party where the kids opened their gifts, and we celebrated the Christmas story. The whole family tried to keep the night as positive as we could. I was near tears the entire evening, but somehow, through the encouragement of the family and leaning heavily on God's comfort, I managed to pull it off. My prayer that night was that somehow God would use the few short months we had Andi to heal her heart and soul while protecting her from more abuse. I had come to realize I had to **choose** to believe that God's plan and timing for Andi *and* for us was in His hands. We prayed with heavy hearts and entrusted Andi to God's protection and care. This was not easy, knowing the uncertainty that she faced as a small child. I found myself questioning the truth of the scripture and asking God if He really knew how much I could stand. Like a child crying out to a parent for help to understand, I was silently begging God to help me through this and give me courage to walk on.

We waited all the next day for DSHS to come pick up Andi. I was constantly holding her and could hardly bear to have her out of my sight. Of course, she thrived on all the attention. Both Jeff and I struggled to trust God's ways and His timing. As each doubt would creep in, we'd quote scripture and pray, all the time trying to keep a positive front for Andi.

At 4:50 that evening, the phone rang. My stomach instantly knotted. I wasn't sure I could take that call, assuming it was the caseworker letting us know the details of the pickup. With trembling hands, I said, "Hello, Weisens." I heard a very excited voice on the other end. The caseworker told me the parents had changed their minds and had just signed the appropriate papers relinquishing all rights. Then she said, "Andi is yours. Merry Christmas!"

Words cannot express the emotional flood that came over me at that moment. I didn't know if I should laugh or cry. I've heard it said many times since, "You never know God is all you need until God is all you have." We had given our anxious thoughts and broken hearts to God. Even before the dreaded call finally came, God chose to intervene. That night, we had our second Christmas Eve party. What a difference twenty-four hours can make.

Remember my story about fishing? Let's consider the stories I just shared about our journey compared to fishing. Just about the time I'm getting ready to reel in for the last time and give up on the day, my pole bends, the bell jingles, and the long-awaited fish is finally on. The waiting is forgotten, replaced by the joy of the catch as I shout, "Fish on!" It seems crazy, but when someone asks about my day of fishing, not one time do I mention the long wait, I just talk about the prize.

How do we continue to thrive in the middle of our storm? Keep our poles in the water, change our attitude and focus, and recast our vision. Then take a seat and wait with expectation for God to provide.

You may wonder about our oldest son, Eddie. His story continues to be written. I hope to share more about his journey in my next project.

Chapter 4

WHAT TO DO WHEN YOU FEEL LIKE QUITTING

The LORD is close to the brokenhearted and saves those who are crushed in spirit.
                                                    Psalm 34:18

It amazes me that a person can walk through a day—seemingly without a care in the world—while experiencing an emotional, spiritual, and physical breakdown on the inside. Many Christians have learned to live with their external and internal emotions being completely disconnected. Our culture encourages us to keep up this façade to perpetuate an impossible standard of perfection. How is it we can become such easy prey to this deception? Upon closer inspection, it appears that one can lose their perspective without realizing their true condition—not necessarily in a sudden freefall, but rather a long, slow descent into despair.

Our family had grown to include our youngest, Tyler, who was now two years old. He had come to us as a huge surprise. I mean literally, I thought I had stomach problems. When I was examined by my doctor because of nausea, I found out I was two months pregnant. We were excited although shocked by the news. Andrea was four at the time and delighted to be having a younger sibling. Eddie was eight, struggling and threatened by this new addition to our family.

We found ourselves at an unexpected turning point in our family dynamic. Eddie was in the fifth grade and had recently been expelled from elementary school. We had been on a first-name basis with the school principal the past five years, which included visits to his office almost daily. Eddie had been placed on probation several times during that period. However, this time was different. We were informed this was a permanent expulsion, and we would have to arrange for his schooling elsewhere.

Shortly after, I had all three kids at home with me. Eddie and I had been embroiled in an ongoing battle of wills the entire day. I had just told Eddie to go to his room and stay there until his dad got home. I turned my back and a moment later, Eddie had lifted Tyler up onto the kitchen counter. Andrea began begging Eddie not to hurt him. When I turned, I looked at Eddie and said, "Eddie, get him down right now, and go to your room!" He defiantly squared his shoulders and glared at me. With his jaw clenched, he hissed, "I know how to *hurt* Tyler." My heart rose in my throat and nearly stopped.

Instinctively, I knew I was facing an impossible situation. A boundary had been crossed, and there would be no negotiating. My heart was pounding. I quickly realized the safety of everyone at that moment depended on my next move. Tyler was crying and reaching for me. Andi was sobbing and screaming at Eddie! In the middle of all this craziness, I felt totally helpless. I begged God to help me in a desperate, silent plea I hoped He could hear above the chaos. I reached for Eddie and Tyler, while at the same time trying to move Andi out of harm's way. Everything seemed in slow motion as the surreal scene unfolded.

It might have been the look in my eye, or perhaps the frantic sound of my voice, but Eddie darted out of arm's reach as I grabbed Tyler into my arms. With two kids clutching me and sobbing, Eddie ran down the stairs and I heard the door slam with a final crash as he shut himself in his room.

My mind was spinning as the questions and doubts began to run rampant. I remember praying, "God, thank you that Tyler wasn't hurt. Oh God, please don't let Andi have more nightmares." An eerie quiet filled the room as I walked to the phone and called Jeff at work. When he answered, I said, "I'm **done!** I can't take this anymore. Get Eddie out of this house." Just writing these words now, years later, gives me chills and brings the bile up in my throat.

Both Jeff and I realized something had to be done, for the sake of everyone. I had no answers for all the questions that flooded my mind: How can a child be so wounded in their first five years of life that they become scarred and can never recover? How is it possible for our family to get so out of control and seemingly hopeless? How on earth did we get to this point? Where is God in all this mess, and why did He ever allow us to adopt Eddie? Didn't God realize we could not survive this? Where are You, God? I kept thinking, if God knows how much we can bear, where *is* He, because I've totally come to the end of my endurance. I am finding it hard to believe that You are close to the brokenhearted. My spirit is crushed.

Looking back, I realize part of our problem was that it had been three years since we'd had any respite from the challenges with the kids because *no one* could or would watch all three kids. Unfortunately, we were oblivious to what was happening. Eddie would play us against each other when he couldn't have his way, followed by some form of acting out—usually something destructive. He then would stand back, blame his sister, and watch as she would take the fall for his act. Andi had begun to withdraw to the extent she would admit to having done things she had not done. She tried to avoid *any* conflict by taking the blame herself. All this time, we thought Andi was causing the issues when it was Eddie the entire time. What a mess our situation had become. It was disturbing at best.

Eddie was such a handful that we could no longer ask Jeff's parents to watch the kids even for a couple hours. He had become increasingly violent and aggressive toward everyone, except Jeff. This fact alone had kept our situation from coming off the rails. Up until this time, Eddie still had a natural fear of, or respect for, Jeff. He did not appear to want to test the limits with Jeff. However, *everything* changed that day.

Jeff and I made one of the hardest decisions of our lives. We called the Child Protective Services (CPS) office and asked for help. We found ourselves in a desperate situation. We could not take a chance of having something happen to *any* of the kids, especially when faced with a threat over which we might or might not have any control. CPS sent a caseworker to the house a *few days* later. When she arrived to assess our situation, she "discovered" she had left the paperwork on her desk. Jeff quickly explained our situation and insisted she leave and return with the paperwork before something tragic happened. A couple of hours later, with information in hand, the caseworker left after telling us they would get back to us. The call came a few days later, letting us know they had found a placement for Eddie.

As it happened, Jeff left for a conference in Seattle on the day they were to come for Eddie. I felt dreadful all morning. I was feeling very sorry for myself and just wanted to quit everything. I was alone as I waited to send Eddie with the caseworker—not knowing when or if we'd ever have him back. I was desperately trying to trust God and believe He was working things out for everyone, but I was failing miserably.

When the caseworker arrived, I was very emotional. I did my best to explain to Eddie that we were not sending him away because we didn't love him, but that we believed he needed more help than we could give. As I knelt by the car saying goodbye, I remember his words to me as though it were yesterday. "Mom, stop crying. Don't worry. You were not a very good mom anyway, and I never really loved you and Dad." He rolled up the window, and they drove away. Just like that, it was over. Eddie, at ten years of age, had been through more than most people experienced in a lifetime. *No* child should ever have to face that. My heart was broken.

There I was, sitting on the porch, sobbing and wanting to quit. I cried out to God that I needed Him, and so did my kids. As I sat there lamenting over the past four-and-a-half years and all that had happened in our home, I was overcome with grief. I continued to beg God to show Himself to me.

In the depths of my heartache, God, in His infinite wisdom, taught me a life lesson that remains with me today. Only the Creator of the universe can redeem a desperate soul in circumstances I believed were *so* out of control.

As I was weeping, I became aware of a noise—peculiar, yet familiar—coming from inside the house. I wiped away my tears and listened carefully. I recognized the sound as the voice of Tyler calling my name, "Mommy! Mommy!" I was shocked. With all that had happened, I forgot about Tyler asleep in his crib. Until that day, Tyler had never climbed out of his crib by himself. I reached for the front door and realized he not only had climbed out of his crib, but had somehow turned the small button on the knob and locked the door. Andi was at school, so there was no one inside the house to help. He was locked in, and I was locked out with no key.

Unable to call for help, because this was long before cell phones, I frantically tried to find a way to get back into the house. I checked all the doors and windows, and nothing was open. I ran back to the front porch and tried to explain to my toddler how to unlock the door. I remember thinking to myself, "Why is it so easy for a two-year-old to lock a door and impossible for him to unlock it?" And then, **Bam**! It hit me. God had my full, undivided attention.

I was completely focused on my "porch" and what *I* had lost thirty minutes before. God had brought me to a point of refocus on what I *still had*. The enemy is very sly with his deceit, and if he can convince us to focus on our loss, he wins. His distraction sucks all energy, motivation, and effectiveness from us as we spiral into a self-centered hole.

Life can have its share of loss, but if we are willing to allow God to use it, He is faithful to remind us how much He still loves us. Yes, Tyler was finally able to unlock the door, and we held each other for a very long time.

Here's the choice: Keep our focus on the "porch" or look up and fix our eyes on Him. Time and again, we will find ourselves forced to take up a position. Just check to make sure it's the correct position—our eyes up and our focus outward. Remember, God is the Creator of *everything* and therefore has a *creative* solution to every problem.

Whenever I feel like quitting, I know it's time to refocus because I usually have all my thoughts, emotions, desires, and dreams centered on myself. Once I look up and look outward, my focus changes, and before long, I can sense God renewing me. My joy is restored, and I'm ready for a new day.

Just recently, our son Tyler shared a quotation he had read online. The unknown writer was sharing about *refocusing*, and used the following:

> *If you have food in your fridge, clothes on your back, a roof over your head, and a place to sleep, you are richer than 75 percent of the world. If you have money in the bank, your wallet, and some spare change, you are among the top 8 percent of the world's wealthy. If you woke up this morning with more health than illness, you are more blessed than the million people who will not survive this week. If you have never experienced the danger of battle, the agony of imprisonment or torture, or the horrible pangs of starvation, you are*

luckier than 500 million people alive and suffering. If you can read this message, you are more fortunate than three billion people in the world who cannot read it at all.

This is a reality check for each of us. Do you need to refocus? Don't delay. Look up now and expect God to meet your gaze. You have to choose to refocus and then practice, practice, practice.

Chapter 5

WHY, WHY, WHY

I have been blessed to be in Christian ministry for over forty years. During this time, the question I've been asked the most is, "Why is this happening to me?" Many times, people are desperate for answers to explain why they, or someone they know and love, have suffered some tragedy or injustice. The question often seems to fall on deaf ears and leaves them grasping at anything they feel makes sense. It is easy to blame someone or something, and God becomes a convenient and safe target.

My experience has taught me that we often ask the wrong question. I know this because I have done the same. It is a safe assumption that everyone, at some point, has heard that when our faith is tested, our character and endurance have an opportunity to grow. Sound familiar?

Consider it pure joy, my brothers and sisters, whenever you face trials of many kinds, because you know that the testing of your faith produces perseverance. Let perseverance finish its work so that you may be mature and complete, not lacking anything (Jms. 1:2–4).

As we read this, we see the words and try to comprehend their meaning and application to our lives. Still, doesn't the same question always surface ... Why? Why doesn't God have a better plan for my character and endurance? Why is this happening? How long before perseverance is finished? There are already hundreds of books available that address why bad things happen to good people, so I'd like to take a different approach.

I have found that memorizing scripture is the *most effective* weapon available to us to face any unexpected twist or turn life sends our way. This has been time-tested and proven true over and over in my life. However, I want to share another tool I have learned to use in dealing with life's trials and its uncertainties.

While raising my daughter, Andi, a typical day went like this for me. "Andi, why did you lie to me?" or "Why did you hide your report card from me?" "Why did you hide your books?" "Andrea Suzanne, I just don't understand you. Why do you constantly make the same poor decisions?" "Why can't I trust you?" And the list got longer.

Have you ever asked these questions as a parent? They all begin with a *Why*. I was trying to raise a fifteen-year-old daughter who was extremely talented and brilliant in many ways. She was a gifted, natural speed reader and a young lady who was more creative than I could fathom. She and

I struggled to find any common ground. I tended to see everything in a positive light, while Andi questioned and seemed to choose the negative. I prayed to God every day to give me direction and wisdom to raise her to love Him and seek Him, but I had a great fear that my struggles in raising her were turning her off to anything spiritual. My constant disappointment in her was growing daily and became harder and harder to conceal. I knew she sensed my disappointment and it hurt her deeply. I felt helpless to pretend her actions were not tearing me apart, and I failed miserably in my attempts to find something positive to say to her.

After months of failure and discouragement, I reached out to my good friend, Ginny Thompson, who had been a teacher for many years. I asked her advice on how best to get through to Andi. As we sat together, I explained my situation and how Andi and I were struggling and not seeming to get anywhere. Ginny listened to me, then began to smile. Honestly, that did *not* make me happy. Here I was, pouring my heart out to her and she was looking at me as if there were no problems in the world. Finally, with extreme irritation in my voice I said, "Ginny, *stop* smiling and tell me what I should do."

She reached out, took both my hands, and rocked my world with her next statement. "Deb, first of all, *stop* asking your daughter why. Just make a voluntary decision right now to never ask her why again." I sat there thinking to myself, "*Why* would I do that?"

Ginny then asked me what answer I got when I asked Andi "why." I said, "It's always the same answer: I don't know. That drives me crazy, and it makes me want to drag it out of her." Ginny said, "*That's* the problem. You start every conversation by putting her on the defensive." I thought back, remembering moments with the kids when they were little. Every question they asked started with, "Why?" At first, it was sweet and adorable. After a time, it became annoying. I was then taken to conversations I'd had with Jeff that started with, "Deb, why did you do that?" I could feel the defenses spring up in my own spirit, just remembering how much I'd wanted to tell him, "**I. Don't. Know!**" I was beginning to understand how this had to be affecting my relationship with Andi.

Ginny then suggested that I stop trying to catch Andi in her lies. *What?* That was one of my best tricks, or at least I thought it was. For instance, if I knew something had happened at school, instead of asking her about it, I'd say, "Sweetheart, did anything happen at school today?" When she answered with a "no," I would start with, "*Why* did you just lie to me?" Ginny explained that not only had I immediately put Andi in a defensive position, but I had also set her up to trap her. Goodness, how did I get to this point? What book had I forgotten to read that could teach me these basic parenting tips?

Well, at the end of our discussion, Ginny and I came up with a plan for Andi and me. The plan was so simple, you'll probably say to yourself, "Duh, that's a no-brainer." I would take Andi on a walk after school for a minimum of fifteen minutes. I would set ground rules before we left the house. I guess I should say, ground *rule* because there was only one rule: She talked, I listened. I was *not* to ask questions or even comment.

I went home excited to try this experiment with my daughter. I told her about the plan, and she rolled her eyes. "Seriously? It will never work." The following day after she got home from school, we reviewed the ground rule and walked out the front door. After fifteen minutes of silence, we went home and went our separate ways. We were to walk three times a week. Wednesday rolled around and I was excited to see if we could make progress. We walked for about twenty minutes and the only words spoken were, "Mom, this is killing you, isn't it?" Little did she know...

I got up Friday morning, begging God for a breakthrough. What I found amazing was that my own spirit was softening toward my daughter and I hadn't even realized it. When Andi walked in after school, she came to the kitchen and said, "Mom, you ready to go?" With renewed hope I said, "You bet!" For the next thirty minutes, Andi walked *and* talked. I mean we barely got off the front porch and she started chatting about her day. Although it started out with just the "stuff" of the day, it ended with her pouring out her heart. By the grace of God, I stayed quiet and did nothing but listen. As the weeks continued, our conversations became blessed, and our relationship healed from the inside out. And yes, I finally got to speak.

During this entire time, Andi was going through her "Goth" phase. She wore black fingernail polish, black lipstick, and had colored her hair black. I would cringe when she would walk into church. I just *knew* everyone thought we were the worst parents. Truthfully, I had been ashamed of her before those walks began. Through the simple act of listening, I came to understand her choices and began to parent for my daughter's health and well-being instead of *my* reputation. Today, twenty-five years later, Andi and I love to walk and talk and share our lives. I am blessed to have a daughter who challenges me and always thinks the best of and for me. We have cried together and forgiven each other for past choices, words, and actions. More importantly, we've both learned *anyone* can live a good life when there is no struggle, but it takes courage to walk through the dark times holding fast to your faith. I believe *that* is what James meant—hold *fast* because the rewards are priceless.

We often hear sermons and read great writings exhorting us to find joy in all circumstances. Being an extremely competitive person, I like to keep the goal in focus. When I think about my struggles, I want to view them with an end in sight. I accept that the journey will be difficult, and I could experience suffering, but I do *not* accept that the struggle will be in vain. I try to no longer ask why, I ask *how*. "How can I get to the finish line," as opposed to "Why is it so hard to get to the finish line?" There is a subtle but *huge* difference. When I ask a different question, or seek to find the question behind the question, my perspective can totally change.

I have often wondered why an all-powerful God doesn't intervene more quickly. Now, I try to turn that question into how I can be thankful for the *entire* journey. I get excited about my own growth and realize that as I grow, those around me often begin to thrive and grow as well.

I have experienced transformation through the testing of my faith. Learning the truth about suffering and trials— that they *can* have purpose and value—has enabled me to refocus and keep my eye on the goal. No suffering is without hope if I surrender to Him, confess my doubt and fear, and practice living in expectation of deliverance.

Helen Keller said, *Character cannot be developed in ease and quiet. Only through experience of trial and suffering can the soul be strengthened, ambition inspired, and success achieved.* (Goodreads.com, Quotable Quotes, Helen Keller – The Story of My Life, 1903)

Another favorite quote about suffering from Brennan Manning: *Suffering, failure, loneliness, sorrow, discouragement, and death will be part of your journey, but the Kingdom of God will conquer all these horrors. No evil can resist grace forever.* (The Ragamuffin Gospel by Brennan Manning, 1990, Multnomah Books)

I find sometimes, God does not intervene quickly because He will not supersede my free will. At other times, He allows me to experience circumstances over which I have no control. It is in these times I must choose to trust Him completely, believing He knows the bigger picture. I choose to seek God's help. For Andi and me, our relationship grew deeper, stronger, and matured through those years of struggle. We did not give up; we persevered, and our relationship was cemented in love, respect, and acceptance. There *is* a better way. Let perseverance finish its work so that you may be mature and complete, *not lacking anything.* James 1:4

I promise, suffering can bring huge benefits and bring us to a place where we can honestly say, "I lack *nothing.*" Suffering can also remind us to ask a *better question*, which can then cause us to look up and gradually lift our eyes off our troubles. Our part is trusting God and not forgetting to memorize scripture. This collaboration with God will move our trust from a thought to an action. Pick one verse, memorize it, and put it to the test. Once you memorize the verse, practice it over and over so you can then own it. Watch it come to mind automatically exactly when you need it. Declaring God's word in a time of trouble will help us get to where we can say with bold faith, "I lack nothing."

Chapter 6

HAIR TODAY...
GONE TOMORROW

In all these things we are more than conquerors through him who loved us.
                                        Romans 8:37

D r. Ryan stepped back from the examining table and looked at my husband and me, then said, "Do you have any stress in your life?" Without much hesitation, both Jeff and I said in unison, "No, not really."

For the next ten minutes, he asked us questions about our family, our business, and life in general. We answered him honestly and watched the expression on his face change with each question. Finally, he paused and looked at us with a full smile. I simply said, "What?" He laughed and said, "I have never talked to a young couple with more problems in their lives and they tell me they have no stress. You are losing your hair and going bald. You lost your first-born son three years ago. You are expanding your small business by adding an additional location *and* you'll be shorthanded at both locations. Then, of course, there are the two children you have adopted from foster care who are both having difficulty adjusting to their new home. Yet, you both agree you have no stress."

It is incredible that life can sometimes become so overwhelming, we have difficulty distinguishing between the nightmare and reality—insanity and normalcy. We struggle to clear the fog, only to wake up entangled and unable to move. We valiantly fight onward and upward, only to find ourselves no farther than where we began. We accept our perception as normal while continuing the daily routines that leave us emotionally drained and physically exhausted—all without ever pausing to examine our lives. God does not want us to live in such deception.

Consider **Psalm 139:23–24**

> *Search me, O God, and know my heart; test me and know my anxious thoughts. See if there is any offensive way in me and lead me in the way everlasting.*

These words remind us to ask God to search our hearts. I believe with God's divine discernment and His leading, we can live our lives aware of His presence, instead of paralyzed and ineffective. We need to do a daily check to make sure we are still living our lives carefully and with a genuine, sincere heart. Without seeking God's inspection, we will never live as the conquerors He desires us to be.

After listening to the doctor's summary of my life, I had to ask myself how I had arrived at this point. In retrospect, it started a few months earlier when we went to Jeff's ten-year college reunion. I was getting ready for the gathering that evening and blow-drying my hair. I noticed something in the mirror and looked closer. As I leaned toward the mirror, I realized that I was looking at a one-inch bald spot on the right side of my head. I ran out to show Jeff and asked him what it might be. My mom, who was hosting us for the weekend, quickly suggested that I had probably caught my hair in the blow dryer. Well, that certainly made perfect sense. I took a deep breath, returned to the mirror, and found a way to cover the spot with a brush and some hairspray.

Throughout the night, Jeff continued to assure me that my bald spot was *not* showing. He said it was important to help me hide it because he didn't want me to win the award for "Most Hair Loss" in the last ten years. What a guy.

Over the next two months, the bald spot grew larger and then multiplied. I wore a hat for a while, trying to cover them up. I did a good job because, for the most part, only family knew I was struggling. Eventually, all the spots merged into one, and the entire top of my head was *completely* bald. During this difficult time, Jeff's humor often saw me through some dark valleys. Neither one of us will forget one particularly excruciating night.

We attended a special church service in a sanctuary filled with a standing-room-only crowd. Earlier that week I had a biopsy taken of my scalp to see if I might have cancer. We were anxiously awaiting the results. As I listened intently to the speaker, his message touched my heart. He suggested that anyone who needed prayer should come forward. Jeff and I quickly made our way to the front of the church and knelt at the altar. I was wearing a navy-blue straw hat that covered any hint of hair loss, as friends and family gathered around us. Everything was fine until a dear friend knelt beside me and put her arms around my neck. As she did, she inadvertently knocked the hat from my head. I was horrified, and panic ensued. Jeff and my friend fumbled with the hat and managed to quickly get it back in position *on* my head. Did I mention I was horrified? Jeff managed to mash the hat on one side in the process. You may be wondering why I didn't just shave my head and go without covering my head. This glorious event happened *long* before women were courageous enough—or society accepting enough—to show their bald heads in public.

In the thirty seconds it took to remove my hat, mash it, and then get it back in place, I experienced both embarrassment and humor. It's been said the definition of humor is tragedy plus time. The question is, "How much time?" Fortunately, God blessed me with a sensitive funny bone, and this mishap struck it like a gong. There I was, kneeling at the altar with my head in my hands, shaking with stifled laughter. As you can imagine, Jeff felt horrible... until he realized I was laughing and not crying. Then he started to laugh as well. It was a wonder one of us didn't snort out loud. Those around us thought we were weeping, and it seemed to me this only caused them to pray louder. This, in turn, caused another round of stifled laughter. I thought the closing prayer would never come. To this day I don't know how we got out of that situation without anyone realizing we were hysterically laughing. It did serve to remind me that God definitely *must* have a sense of humor.

The next day, I went downtown to a store specializing in hair pieces and purchased a wig. This would prove to be another unforgettable day. I settled into the salon chair to begin trying on wigs. As I numbly gazed in the mirror, I found myself face to face with reality. I fought back tears and felt totally embarrassed to have *everyone* watching me and offering their opinion. I finally chose a wig, as all the gals reassured me my purchase "was *darling*." It did seem to me, though, like it was a *ton* of hair. I choked back my emotions, thanked them, and then went straight to the car, where I completely broke down with my forehead against the steering wheel. When my sobbing subsided, I began to question God. "Lord, how can I do this? When is enough, enough? What are You trying to teach me?"

I made my way home, where Jeff met me at the door. The minute I saw him, I started to sob again and blurted out, "Don't laugh! I know. I look just like Dolly Parton!" Never one to be at a loss for words, he quickly replied, "Uh, sorry, babe, but you still don't look like Dolly Parton." I quickly realized he was not talking about my *big* hair. Once again, Jeff's sense of humor helped me see the silver lining, be it ever so thin. A short time later, I took the scissors to my *big* wig, and trimmed it down to a more reasonable size and style. I began to wear it daily as more and more of what remained of my hair fell out.

My hair loss was a journey for the entire family. I was taking Cortisone shots to help my hair grow back following a diagnosis of Alopecia Areata. Andi, who was eight at the time, was embarrassed and hated when I removed my wig. Tyler, who was four, would pull my wig off as soon as I got home from work, and sit and rub my sore head. Jeff was always encouraging and helping me refocus when I needed it most. Each one of us had to deal the best we could with our doubts, our fear, and our uncertainties.

Ultimately, this is how Romans 8:38–39 became my anchor:

> *For I am convinced that neither death nor life, neither angels nor demons, neither the present nor the future, nor any powers, neither height nor depth, nor* **baldness,** *nor anything else in all creation, will be able to separate us from the love of God that is in Christ Jesus our Lord.*

Looking back years later, I can see how a very vain, young mom would be forever changed through her hair loss. I can also see that God can use *anything* to bring about His will for our lives. I learned what really mattered in this life. I was humbled, and my faith was strengthened as I faced each day, choosing joy and hope over self-pity and despair.

I had days filled with doubts and weakness. Yet those days taught me to lay my pride aside and call on trusted friends to pray for me and encourage me when I needed it most. Those friends saw me through difficult days and today remain bonded to me forever. Some days, I simply struggled to put one foot in front of the other. Other days, I kept walking forward quoting all the scriptures I had memorized, which gave me courage and strength. Psalm 27:1–8 became a constant friend and reminder. I suggest you read it in the Living Bible.

> The Lord is my light and my salvation; he protects me from danger—whom shall I

fear? When evil men come to destroy me, they will stumble and fall. Yes, though a mighty army marches against me, my heart shall know no fear. I am confident that God will save me.

The one thing I want from God, the thing I seek most of all, is the privilege of meditating in his Temple, living in his presence every day of my life, delighting in his incomparable perfections and glory.

There I'll be when troubles come. He will hide me. He will set me on a high rock out of reach of all my enemies. Then I will bring him my sacrifice of praise with singing and with much joy.

Listen to my pleading, Lord. Be merciful and send the help I need. My heart has heard you say, "Come and talk with me, O my people." And ***my heart responds***, "Lord, I am coming."

I was bald for almost two years with little hope of ever having hair again. This experience was one of the toughest tests of my life. The sections of scripture I memorized were a constant help in my efforts to cope and refocus.

One particularly dark day, I was having a severe pity party and felt hopeless and discouraged. Jeff came into the bathroom where I was looking at my bald head in the mirror. He hugged me and tried to encourage me by reminding me that it didn't matter if I had hair or not... yada, yada, yada. Suddenly, he said, "**Holy Cow!**" He left the room and returned shortly, carrying my nine-year-old scrub brush that I used on vegetables. It was an abused, worn-out thing with all the bristles flattened outward in an awkward circular pattern. Can you picture it? He held it up and said, "Babe, check this out. On the top of your head, there's a new patch of soft, white hair that looks just like this brush."

I punched him and then sheepishly looked for myself. Sure enough, it was just as he said—soft and white, and about a half inch long. We hugged again, and I had a good, thankful cry as we celebrated. That day marked the beginning of the regrowth of *all* my hair. It came in with new color, very curly *and* very thick. Every hair on my head is a gift, and God knows the exact number. (Luke 12:7)

I learned so much about myself through that journey. It was very personal and challenged everything that I thought was important. My appearance, my self-worth, my entire well-being was centered on how I looked and what other people thought. It wasn't until I chose to thank God for my baldness that *I* began to change. Once I made that choice, my outlook and my self-worth began to be shaped into something much more usable and genuine. The vanity that had subtly taken over who I was began to be demolished. My idol of self-awareness shattered. My joy returned long before my hair did. That is important, because without my joy, I was of no use to my family or friends.

Hair today, gone tomorrow. I want to close this chapter by asking a few questions. What have you allowed to separate you from the love of God? What keeps you from being a conqueror? Is it a broken relationship, a word spoken against you that will not leave you alone? A job loss? A broken romance, addiction, discouragement, self-pity or even prosperity? What idol have you chosen that may need to be brought down and shattered? If you're missing the joy in your journey, ask God to search *your* heart. As God carefully and lovingly molds you through trials, and if you continue to surrender, He can literally make beauty from ashes.

Would you rather live in praise or despair? I can tell you with certainty that God promises to see you through whatever you face when you turn to Him and ask Him to take the ashes of your life and remake them into His vision for you. Seeking God must become the most important part of your day.

We are more than conquerors through Jesus Christ, and the power to live daily in His love is available to those who will choose it.

Choose well, my friends.

> *Be very careful, then, how you live—not as unwise but as wise, making the most of every opportunity, because the days are evil* (Eph. 5:15–16).

Chapter 7

SETBACK OR COMEBACK?

*Being confident of this, that he who began a
good work in you will carry it on to completion until the day of Christ Jesus.*

Philippians 1:6

A SENIOR MOMENT

I wonder how many reading this book have for just one
moment thought they might have a child who could one
day be in the NBA. I think the statistic is something like
0.03 percent of players make it from high school to the NBA.

Growing up, Tyler was an average athlete, but he had
above-average self-discipline. When faced with any challenge, he never shied away and usually met the challenge

with great success. Tyler was obsessed with basketball. Jeff and I took great joy in watching him compete and found ourselves planning life around Tyler's basketball opportunities.

After his sophomore year of high school basketball, his future was looking very bright. However, that summer during summer ball, we noticed that Ty seemed a little tentative when given an opportunity to shoot the ball. At first, we were a little concerned, and encouraged him to be more selfish with the ball. Can you imagine a parent telling her child to be selfish? Ugh ... It's hard to admit how much we wanted him to succeed.

His junior year was not phenomenal, and yet through hard work and self-discipline he was physically becoming stronger, and that alone was making a difference in his game. The following summer before his senior year as we watched him play, his dad and I became more and more concerned about his hesitations. Something was not quite right. We just could not put our finger on it. It was like he would overthink every shot. Those couple of seconds began to affect his entire game.

We also noticed that when not playing ball, he was easily distracted while in conversation. It felt at times like he would just zone out and quit talking. After a bit he would come back to the conversation and re-engage, sometimes asking what we were talking about. He developed some good skills at covering, but it was becoming more and more obvious at home that something more was going on with Tyler.

After much discussion with Tyler, we decided to take him to a neurologist. We discovered that he was having petit mal seizures. After further testing, it was confirmed that Tyler had epilepsy. He began medication immediately, and it helped with the seizures and his concentration. The petit mals never completely went away, but he learned to adequately cover them up and develop a normal routine. However, the strong medicine made him lethargic, and playing basketball at a competitive level became impossible. As a result, he was now faced with an entirely new set of challenges.

Imagine a senior in high school having to give up the sport he loved and had poured his life into for the past eleven years. On top of that, the doctor took Tyler's license away for six months because of the seizures. That was supposed to give him time to adjust to his new medication, which meant most of his senior year he could not drive at all.

Jeff and I were devastated for him and questioning God's plan and direction for our son. We tried to encourage Tyler the best we could, reminding him how much more there was to life besides basketball. It sounds almost trite, but it is so true. We continued to remind him to trust God. All the while, we both fought the disappointment we felt and knew Tyler must feel also. We believed that God could touch Tyler, yet God's presence seemed so distant and His voice mute. We were saying all the right things, but deep down we questioned God and His plan for our son. It was easy to verbalize what we knew to be truth, but quite another to live it out day to day, especially when it involved our own son. Once again, every morning we had to choose to trust and direct our focus specifically on God and the knowledge He was in control of Tyler's life, as well as ours.

We held a family meeting to formulate a schedule plan to get Tyler everywhere he needed to be, knowing he could no longer drive himself. It was a miserable meeting because honestly, I just wanted to scream at God and ask Him, "Why Tyler?" How quickly I had fallen back into the old habit of asking *why* instead of *how*. I was fighting back tears when Ty turned to me and said, "Mom, *stop*! I've had such an awesome life. I've loved basketball so I can't wait to see what God has next for me. Also, transportation *will not* be a problem. I'll reach out to my friends, and they will help me get around and will probably even double date with me so they can drive. They are a bunch of great guys, so stop worrying. It will all work out. We just have to trust God."

Yeah, like *he* said. How do you say ... **Busted**!

I must admit I was enjoying the *other* plan—my plan—where we watched him play basketball and dreamed about his future in the sport. And here is another thought. How many seventeen-year-olds have friends who would do all that for them? Lastly, when did he become so wise?

I sat in my chair listening to Tyler share his perspective, and this mom was humbled and brought to her knees. After all the years of struggle with our family, finally being able to celebrate some successes did not seem like too much to ask. Yet, here was my son reminding *me* that he'd had a great life and was thankful for all the opportunities basketball had given him. He had to remind us that God was *not* finished with him yet. I realized that somehow all those life lessons we'd been trying to teach had stuck, and this young, godly man would be just fine. That evening I also realized that Tyler would be more than fine, he'd be victorious regardless of his circumstances. Thank God. He used Tyler to remind me that *my* God is *enough*.

Tyler never really looked back, just picked up with his new normal, and even became one of the best cheerleaders for his own basketball team. At games you could often hear him above everyone else.

What the enemy chose as a huge setback for Tyler and our family, God and Tyler used as one of the biggest comebacks of his life. He helped us see that our Plan B is *not* God's plan. Tyler's life verse has always been Philippians 1:6.

Being confident of this, that he who began a good work in you will carry it on to completion until the day of Christ.

Tyler's struggle with epilepsy did not go away. In his first year at college, he experienced his first grand mal seizure. His petit mal seizures had become a constant companion throughout every single day, interfering with his normal routine. They affected his studies, especially when presenting business plans and proposals for course requirements in front of the class. He continued to move forward, doing his best to keep his disease in check, though thoughts of *another* seizure were always present in the back of his mind. It was a constant struggle for him. However, Tyler would not allow it to control his life. He spent the summer following his junior year in England, coaching basketball and running camps for underprivileged kids in the local schools.

As parents, we constantly faced the fear of "what ifs," which kept us praying and trusting God while Tyler pursued his dreams.

Upon returning from England, he fought through his final year and graduated, despite an ongoing battle with the strong epilepsy medications. As a family, we continued to pray for a miracle and believed that God could *and* would touch Tyler's body *and* his life.

Following college, Tyler moved with friends to the Seattle, Washington, area where they lived and worked together as young millennials seeking their dreams. They loved the big-city life and enjoyed its amenities. Eventually, life took them in different directions, each with new opportunities. Tyler returned to Spokane, where he continued to work. In the meantime, he still struggled with his medication and its side effects. His doctor persisted in trying to find the right combination of drugs to provide Tyler with the ability to function and communicate effectively with his clients and fellow workers. We had no clue that a coming change for us, would be the answer to Tyler's seizures.

Out of the blue, a college friend who pastored a church in Vancouver, Washington, called and wanted to know if I would move to Vancouver and become his associate pastor. We had played on the college golf team together and had remained friends since that time. When he called, I was very happy with my current job and declined the offer. Spokane was home and we planned to retire there. However, my "no" did not dissuade him, and he continued to stay in touch throughout the summer. After many calls back and forth, Jeff and I decided to take a trip to meet with him and his wife Jan and check out the church during the upcoming Labor Day weekend.

I had fully intended to say, "Thank you, but no thank you." However, the weekend was a delightful time of renewed friendship as well as making new friendships. As we reflected on the possibilities of this new adventure on our return home, we decided to put out a fleece while praying and fasting to help us determine exactly what God wanted us to do. Following several days of praying and fasting, neither of us felt a definite yes or no. We would be leaving life-long friends, family, our church, *and* a printing business we had owned for thirty-four years. We were comfortable, established, and content with our lives. Yet, what if God had a bigger and better plan in mind for us? We didn't want to miss some indicator of God's will in this decision.

Surprisingly, we had an incredible peace about this new opportunity and decided to take the first step together through what appeared to be an open door. We prayed earnestly that God, in His infinite wisdom, would slam the door shut if this move was not His will for us at this time. When we chose to surrender our lives, we were then able to move forward with a new excitement and anticipation. We compiled a list of over thirty "miracles" that we needed to take place in chronological order for us to be able to make the move. One by one we began to check each one off the list. It was absolutely remarkable. We keep that list today as a reminder of all God did for us.

On October 28, 2011, we stood on our deck overlooking our six acres, with our horses looking up at us for the last time. We thanked God for the years we'd spent there. We emotionally surrendered our future to Him and climbed into the two U-Haul trucks. We still had to say goodbye to our daughter as we left town and that proved to be heart-wrenching.

Little did we know how God would orchestrate His will in our decision, and what role that would play in changing Tyler's life forever. Tyler decided to move with us to the greater Portland/Vancouver area, as he had always wanted to return to the Pacific coast and the alure of the big city.

This move required him to find a new neurologist. It proved a difficult task, as his doctor was unable to provide a referral and none of us were familiar with anyone who could offer one. Tyler picked a neurologist from a list provided by a Google search and scheduled an appointment after learning the doctor would accept his insurance. Tyler liked the doctor immediately. During the first appointment, the doctor informed him he thought Tyler was on the wrong medication. He told him that he needed a different drug, along with an additional medication.

On his way home, Tyler picked up the new meds and within days of taking the new prescription, his petit mal seizures appeared completely under control. I mean, *completely*! That was ten years ago, and he has yet to experience another petit mal. Oh, he *still* has epilepsy and has since had an additional grand mal, but his daily life is completely different now that he can focus and maintain clear thought processes.

All through high school and college, Tyler dreaded speaking in front of crowds because of his epilepsy. Today, he is a marketing director and trainer for a financial firm and has many opportunities to speak in front of large groups. Often, he is stopped after a presentation and congratulated on his delivery and enthusiasm. Motivational speaking has become one of Tyler's strengths. His passion for helping people has given him many opportunities to pour his life into others.

I believe things may have turned out very differently for Tyler had he never had that view from the porch when he was six years old. Through experiences and circumstances beyond his control, during which he had to surrender his life and his dreams to God, Tyler has learned how to trust the One who knew him before he was born. I continue to learn from Tyler as I watch him grow and mature. He consistently looks up and lives with expectations and enthusiasm, no matter his circumstances.

During the COVID-19 pandemic in 2020, John Maxwell reminded us during an online presentation that there are "players and pretenders." He said that a crisis reveals which you are. Pretenders are those in a basketball game who want to throw the ball in when there are ten seconds left. Players are those who want to receive the ball and attempt the final shot. Tyler has chosen to be a player. I hope you are choosing to do likewise.

Do you ever find yourself living vicariously through your children? I challenge you to remember this is *their* life story. The best advice I can give is to understand that when a setback comes into your life, *they* are watching *you*. Hopefully, as they watch your reactions and choices, they will be learning to have strong foundations and values of their own. John Maxwell says to *fail forward*. I promise, you may not always do it right, but if you are willing to admit failure and learn from it, your children will learn what true success is.

Tyler continues to hold fast to his life verse:

> *Being confident of this, that he who began a good work in you will carry it on to completion until the day of Christ Jesus* (Phil. 1:6).

This has allowed his life's biggest test to become his testimony.

Chapter 8

LOOKING UPWARD

"For my thoughts are not your thoughts, neither are your ways my ways," declares the LORD. "As the heavens are higher than the earth, so are my ways higher than your ways and my thoughts than your thoughts."

Isaiah 55:8–9

Over twenty-five years ago, while attending a children's pastor's conference, I had arrived late to the day's luncheon in the conference center. I was looking for a seat, when a voice said, "Young lady, are you looking for a place to sit?" The only seat available in the immediate vicinity was next to the man whose voice I had heard. We introduced ourselves, and he invited me to attend his sports ministry workshop to learn more about reaching my community for Christ through sports. His name was Caz McCaslin, the founder of Upward Sports, a nationwide sports ministry based in Spartanburg, South Carolina. That day began a friendship that has lasted to this day and grown richer through the years. Some might say we met by chance, but Caz and I believe it was a God-ordained moment.

The Upward Sports Basketball and Cheerleading program was a perfect fit for our church. It grew over the years and expanded to include four churches across our community all working together. Our church was led by a pastor who lived and breathed "outreach" to those in the community, and he encouraged all of us to do likewise. I found myself looking for opportunities to share my faith in every part of my day. There was nothing routine or mundane anymore, just expectations for new opportunities each morning. I lived the words of Paul in his letter to the Philippians 2:2 "By being like-minded, having the same love, being one in spirit and of one mind." The connections and "assignments" God continued to give me in our community increased, and I was finding great joy in ministry and outreach every day. God's impact on my spiritual growth, and that of our entire church body, was exhilarating.

Shortly after we had completed the tenth year of Upward Basketball and Cheerleading—the largest outreach program of our church and one of the largest children's sporting opportunities in our community—our pastor retired after twelve years at the helm. Up to this point, my whole being was found in encouraging children and their families to get to know Jesus. I rarely went into a grocery store or mall without being stopped by someone and questioned about Upward. I could not imagine doing anything else.

Church leadership hired a new pastor who brought to the church a different vision centered on preaching and teaching. The outreach programs were re-evaluated and prioritized to align with that vision. I had served my church as a lay pastor on staff for twenty-four years and was beginning to sense God leading me in a different direction. Pastor Bob Luhn, a good friend, had once told me that if I found myself serving without joy, my ministry was probably completed. I found myself in that exact spot—serving had somehow become a duty.

Sometime later, I received a call from Caz, checking in to see how things were going. During the conversation, I asked him to pray for me as I began to earnestly seek God's direction, strength, and help to stay focused on my responsibilities as Family Life Director. I continued to pour myself into the families and people of our church and community while praying for courage and endurance to stay true to God's will and purpose for my life.

I found myself talking to God, searching His Word daily, and listening for the Spirit's discernment. At the same time, I desperately wanted God to rescue me out of my struggle. Nothing happened. I thought maybe God wanted me to stay put and trust Him. Sometimes, the *hardest* thing to do is to "be *still*, and *know* He is God." Ps. 46:10

We took a much-needed vacation break to Hawaii. Our hope was to refresh, refocus, and return encouraged to stay the course. Our time away included lots of hikes to waterfalls and walks on the beach, which gave me plenty of time for reflection and introspection. I felt completely at peace and ready to return home.

While coming back from our final hike on the last day of vacation, my phone rang, showing a South Carolina

864 area code. I answered the call and was shocked when I heard, "Hey, Deb, this is Priscilla from Upward. We would like you to come to Spartanburg and interview for a position coming available in your territory. Could you be on a flight this Thursday if we booked it for you?"

I had no hesitation or doubt about it. I had been praying and knew immediately that God was moving. He hears us when we call on Him (1 John 5:15). He reminds us to seek His face, and in doing so, we know Him when He calls us. Jeff was already giving me the thumbs up, so I said, "I'll make that work."

We flew home the next day, and I left for Spartanburg the following day. It is about a twelve-hour flight, making for a very long travel day. I got in at 11:00 p.m. and, of course, my luggage did *not* arrive with me. My interview was at 8:00 a.m. the next day, and I was dressed in a t-shirt, jeans, and flip-flops while traveling. At 6:00 the next morning I still had not received my luggage from the airlines. I jumped into my rental car in search of the nearest Walmart. I purchased some cosmetics, a curling iron, a nice shirt and a jean skirt, and hurried back to the hotel to get ready for the interview. To say I was a bit *stressed* would be an enormous understatement.

I interviewed with several people, which took most of the day. I was told that I would hear about the position by the middle of next week. I arrived at the airport later that same day and finally connected with my luggage. Then I settled into a seat to wait for my flight. I had only been sitting there a few minutes when my phone rang. I answered and heard, "Deb, this is Priscilla. We couldn't wait until next week to offer you the position as our new representative for the twelve western states. Welcome to Upward,

Deb!" I sat there very calmly fighting the tears while letting her know I was thrilled to accept the position. When we hung up, I remember closing my eyes and soaking in God's goodness and His incredible design for my life. Just weeks before, I had been at my wits' end, wondering if I would be able remain in my position at the church. Once more, I found that by trusting and waiting on God and His plan in His time, He opened an opportunity that would completely restore my *joy* in serving. The great Creator had created an even larger window through which I would see *His* plan and have a much greater impact than I could imagine.

My passion for leading children and their families to the Savior continued to intensify as I followed His leading. He allowed this unique ministry to expand from our one church to five more in our community, and then explode to over one hundred churches across the western United States. One of my special friends from Lodi, California, recently wrote me this email:

> *"Hey Deb,*
> *I hope all is well with you. It's hard to believe, but we will be starting our 10th season of Upward in Lodi, CA. Each year continues to grow. Last season we had nearly 1,000 kids participating in basketball and cheer, and we are now partnering with 3 other churches in town. First Baptist of Lodi is thriving! Also, to date, our snack bar has raised about $60,000 for clean water projects in Lesotho, Africa. For a little town of 75,000 in Northern California, Upward has become one of the premiere sports leagues.*

*Thank you, for your leadership and encour-
agement over the years!"*
Dr. Eric Larson

Have you ever kept God in a box and unintentionally
allowed fear and doubt to creep in and replace your joy? If
you have, then ask God to help you open the box you've
put Him in and enlarge your vision. You'd better hold on
because that's exactly what He will do. God allowed me to
minister to a church of 600, but even then, He had a bigger
plan. He led me to an opportunity to share His love with
thousands.

I hope to inspire you to remember that God is so much
bigger than you can begin to imagine. His ways are not our
ways, and He is never hindered by time and space. His
thoughts are not our thoughts, and He provides beyond
anything you can dream or imagine.

Make the decision to follow Him with expectations of
a vibrant new day, a new way, and an exciting new challenge.

Chapter 9

AIRPORTS ARE *NOT* FOR SISSIES

> *You do not have because you do not ask God.* When you ask, you do not receive, because you ask with **wrong motives**, that you may spend what you get on your pleasures.
> James 4:2–3

O ver the span of my life, I have learned that one of my biggest struggles comes from my negative self-talk. You may know what I am talking about. I have a discussion with myself that, if left unchecked, can lead down a rabbit hole of negativity, leaving me stuck and frustrated in a whirlpool of doubt. It's that conversation that swirls around in my head and will *not* stop. The subject usually has to do with *my* integrity, *my* selfishness or maybe an injustice

I feel. It can be, at times, when I say to myself, "It's not fair!" or, "I'm not enough!" and basically beat myself up because I am totally focused on me, myself, and I.

When I think about why I allow this self-talk to overwhelm me, there are three reasons that become apparent as I look at James 4:2–3.

First, I do not ask God to fulfill the desires of my heart. Instead, I often manipulate my circumstances to get what I want—that need or desire that *consumes* me. Second, when I *do* ask, I have the *wrong* motive, usually a selfish one. Third, I become so self-absorbed that I forget I am to be an example for those around me who may be watching. This is clearly stated in Titus 2:7, *"In everything set them an **example** by doing what is **good**."*

So, how *do* I find that balance and use my God-given ability for rational thought and stop the negative thinking? How *do* I shut off this cycle of discontentment and lack of self-control that consumes my mind? How *can* I create a stronger and more consistent lifestyle by living full of joy and maintaining healthy thoughts?

Often the answer is simple, yet difficult because it means I must take action and *not* allow myself to stay stuck. First, I confess and admit that what I am doing is wrong. If I want to live with integrity, being vulnerable and genuine, I *must* stop the cycle of negative thinking. If I cannot overcome this negative self-talk, then when given an opportunity to shine my light as an example of God's love, I will surely fall short.

Second, when it comes to my motives, I must be honest about what is driving my negative thoughts.

Jeremiah 17:9 says, *The heart is deceitful above all things, and desperately sick; who can understand it?*

When I am willing to examine my heart, God will show me the true motives by unveiling my eyes to the truth. Admitting the possibility that I'm not being honest with myself and then asking for God's help to understand my hidden motives can help set my swirling thoughts free. That is just the plain, ugly truth—my heart is deceitful and no amount of wishing it otherwise will fix it. I can tell you that being real with God and asking Him to peel back the layers of my pride and selfishness is very difficult at times, but necessary if I want Him to purify my heart. God is a God of mercy and love, and *His* desire to guide me gives me the courage to allow myself to be teachable and moldable. Asking the Holy Spirit to search me daily and show me where I am offensive and anxious helps me trust Him to grow my faith and allows me to persevere in my walk. Also, it is my way to remain pure with my motives, even those I may not know I have.

Search me, O God, and know my heart; test me and know my anxious thoughts. See if there is any offensive way in me and lead me in the way everlasting (Ps. 139:23–24).

By the way, if I don't ask God to search me, I guarantee someone close to me will do the searching and I will *not* like what they find. However, here's some great news. The Holy Spirit will help me overcome my *stinkin' thinkin'* with some effort and perseverance on my part. It makes such a difference to be able to boldly approach God with my heart's desire when *my* will lines up with *His* will and I ask with a pure heart. We can know He hears us and will answer when we call out to Him. Expect God to effect miraculous changes when you open your heart's door to Him.

Third, when my heart and mind begin to entertain a negative thought, I must remember that my true character is *who I am when no one is watching.* You've probably seen or heard this simple object lesson: A person is holding a glass of water. They ask, "If I shake this glass, what will come out of it?" That's right ... water. Whatever is filling our hearts *will* come out when we are shaken. It will have a sweet fragrance, or it will be bitter and nasty.

This is a great reminder to live by the power of the Spirit, and *in step* with Him, as Paul reminds us in Galatians 5:25. I don't want to get out ahead of the Spirit, nor do I want to lag behind, but remain in lockstep with Him every moment of every day. When I pursue this kind of daily walk with God, I need not fear what may spill out when I am faced with circumstances that may shake my heart.

You and I are to be living sacrifices, and this means being ready at *any* time to be used by God. We *never* know when or how He may place us in someone's path to make a difference in that person's life. Only God knows. We are to live in step with Him so that we are not caught unaware when a divine appointment is presented. Be ready. Be brave and ask God to use you to share His love. Ask God to make you an example for others to follow. Ask God to humble you and prepare you to do something greater than you've ever imagined.

WARNING! When you become His vessel, God moves in the most unexpected ways. You must be prepared and ready.

It was a special day when I heard God loud and clear. I smiled to myself, marveling at the way He works in my life. My meeting had ended early. I had met with several churches in Las Vegas to talk about starting basketball leagues in local churches, and I was eager to get home. I headed to the airport, hoping to catch an earlier flight. Vegas was not my favorite airport at that time because it seemed like at least one runway was always under construction, which often delayed flights. I checked in and headed to my gate and settled in to begin my usual routine of watching people. After about an hour, I noticed that the airport was really filling up and no one seemed to be taking off. I heard some groans next to me and looked up at the kiosk. I read these dreaded words posted next to my flight number: **Flight Delayed!** Apparently, the wind had come up and they were having some nasty sandstorms. Since one runway was closed, it was impossible to get flights off the ground until the storm passed.

I decided to go get something to eat and settle in for the long wait. Of course, when I came back my seat was taken. I leaned up against a post, which allowed me to look out a long row of floor-to-ceiling windows, and I settled in to eat my lunch. I continued to lean against that pole for the next four hours. The airport was packed with passengers waiting impatiently for flights to resume. Many of the vendors had run out of food, and I could sense the tension in the air. People were reaching their limit of patience and tempers were beginning to flare sporadically. It was fascinating to watch as people became irritable and downright cranky. I was never once offered a place to sit during the long wait, so my own attitude was also in question as I shifted my weight from one side to the other, and back again.

After what seemed like an eternity, I sensed some commotion. My place at the post provided me a great view of the tarmac. I stood a little taller as I watched to get a glimpse of the action below my perch. What happened next is imprinted on my memory as if it were yesterday.

A vehicle pulling two long luggage carts came flying out from under the terminal. I smiled to myself thinking, "Whoa, that guy's hauling."

The vehicle shot across the designated loading area and then made a sharp left turn directly in front of where I was standing. As it made the turn, luggage of all shapes, sizes, and colors flew off both trailers, hit the tarmac, and rolled away in every direction. As I watched the event unfold, I couldn't help but react with a loud, "**Oh!**" At that, literally scores of people sitting or standing by the windows looked my way and then out at the scene below.

A young man jumped off the vehicle, walked behind it, and disappeared. Moments later, luggage appeared in the air sailing up and over one cart only to land in the next empty cart. Some pieces missed their mark, haphazardly falling short or bouncing off the top and rolling off the opposite side. The resulting cascade of luggage became quite comical. I began to snicker and then laugh. As it continued, more and more people began to take notice. Some laughed, but others were unhappy with the way this young man was roughly handling the bags. One man reacted by saying, "That had better not be *my* suitcase or that dude is in *big* trouble." Several others agreed, but the suitcases continued to fly one after another.

Eventually, the young man came around the full carts and began retrieving the bags that had bounced off and landed on the ground on the other side. He was now facing the six large picture windows and all of us as we collectively held our breath. We waited for what might happen next. He grabbed a red case and threw it up on the cart with the others. As he did, his eyes locked with mine, or at least it seemed like they did. He proceeded to scan each window and realized that dozens, if not hundreds, of people were watching every move he made.

The man's next move had a dramatic effect on those of us standing there. He held up both hands as if giving us the STOP signal and ran along the carts displaying this sign to each window in turn. Inside the terminal, people watched and waited quietly. He then proceeded to grab the suitcases remaining on the tarmac and very carefully, and intentionally, placed each one neatly on the carts so as not to repeat the mishap. After replacing about ten bags, he turned and faced all the people staring at him through the window. He then ran along the carts giving everyone a thumbs-up sign, smiling as if he'd won the jackpot.

In an instant, everyone inside began to give him the thumbs-up and cheer for him. The groaning and complaining had quickly turned to laughter and high fives. The young man jumped on his cart and quickly sped away, waving at all of us.

As I boarded the plane, I was amazed at the difference in everyone's demeanor. It was as if that shared moment had made us all friends. People were laughing and sharing other stories and even high fiving me as they went by.

My experience was a simple reminder to me that I *am* contagious and that my daily struggles can *always* be turned to good if I allow God to be involved in my routine. That young driver could have reacted many ways, yet he made the choice to engage with us. It not only saved him from several nasty write-ups, but it also helped a weary group of travelers refocus for just a moment and find a reason to smile. Have you noticed that our character, like our attitude, is contagious?

The apostle Paul gives us a great example of this. While sitting in prison, he penned these words found in Philippians 4:12, *I have learned to be content no matter what the circumstances.* Seriously? While sitting in prison, he talks about contentment.

I waste time complaining, worrying, whining, and griping when I should be living in complete *freedom*— freedom to choose contentment. We must practice choosing to not let our **chains** control our **choices**, even in the routines of a day (i.e., driving a luggage cart, working at a coffee stand, being a stay-at-home mom or a high-powered executive). It doesn't matter what our positions are, it's the daily choices that allow us to give glory to the Father and lead others to take a first, second, or third look at God's plan and purpose for their lives.

This story is a good reminder that the choice is mine and I get to make it every day, and it doesn't end here. On the flight home, I was able to share my faith with the gentleman sitting beside me the entire way to Portland, Oregon. When we parted, he said that for the first time in years, he was going home with some hope.

I do not believe it was just circumstance that placed this man next to me. God opened a door of opportunity because of an experience my fellow traveler and I shared involving an airline baggage handler. We never know how or when an opportunity will arise. Be ready to be an example by doing what is good.

> *In everything set them an **example** by doing what is **good**. In your teaching show integrity, seriousness and soundness of speech that cannot be condemned, so that those who oppose you may be ashamed because they have nothing bad to say about us* (**Tit. 2:7–8 NIV**).

Chapter 10

SPEWED UPON, BUT
NOT FORSAKEN

*Praise be to the God and Father of our Lord
Jesus Christ, the Father of compassion and
the God of all comfort, **who comforts us in
all our troubles, so that we can comfort
those in any trouble with the comfort we
ourselves receive from God.** For just as we
share abundantly in the sufferings of Christ,
so also our comfort abounds through Christ.*
2 Corinthians 1:3–5

On another trip, I found myself in the same Las Vegas
airport when God gave me another clear lesson on
the importance of being ready so I can stand firm in all circumstances. My suffering can help others if I hold steady

and learn to trust God to get me through. I must take up my position in Christ daily and put on His full armor. That way, no matter what the day brings, I stand **ready.** When the unexpected happens, I can choose to be used for His glory or I can allow the unexpected to become a woe-is-me, self-centered event.

The terminal was extremely busy and flights were backed up, making for a two to three-hour wait, at minimum. I just wanted to get home, so I tried to stay busy by reading and writing so the time would pass quickly.

When the boarding call for my flight finally came, I was in the second group to board. It seemed to take *forever* to get down the gangway. The line was backed up to the check-in desk and creeped along at a snail's pace.

Many people were grumbling that those putting their carry-on bags in the overhead bins were taking way too long. I nodded in agreement while thinking to myself, "*Those* people are a big problem." Eventually, I stepped into the plane and was inching my way down the aisle. As the line slowly moved forward, not only was I frustrated, but I found myself stewing in anger. I searched the aisle and surrounding seats for anyone who needed a glare—someone to whom I could give the "hurry up" sign. However, it was an exercise in futility.

After passing a few more rows of seats, I heard laughter and giggling. Passengers seemed to be enjoying themselves and conversations were expressive and lighthearted. The giggling, followed by more laughter, grew louder and seemed to come in waves every time the line moved forward. I quickly found myself wondering what was causing all this commotion. It didn't take long before I witnessed firsthand what was slowing my boarding process.

To my amazement, the cutest one-year-old Asian baby appeared, standing on his mama's lap. His puffy little cheeks were round and appeared ready to burst. He looked like a wide-eyed little chipmunk getting ready for the winter. He held a fistful of fish crackers in his hand, and as each person passed by, he looked up into their eyes and gleefully bubbled out something sounding like, "Kacker?" as he raised his chubby little hand toward their faces. Each person politely responded with, "No, thank you." and laughed as they continued moving, while remarking to those around them about the cute baby.

It was finally my turn to encounter this little time-stealing fish-cracker monster. I was already smiling, but I was not prepared for what happened next. This cute, chubby baby with cheeks stuffed full of orange fish crackers threw his head back and sneezed. His little cheeks simply could hold no more. The explosion of wet, orange cracker debris spewed out, completely covering his mama's face. She had long, beautiful black hair with straight bangs. Her dark eyes were framed with long black lashes, which were now completely covered by the sticky orange mush. Globs of soggy crackers were stuck on her cheeks, too. Basically, she was buried in **yuck!**

An awkward, momentary silence followed as we all heard the baby say clearly, "Uh-oh!" You could have heard a pin drop as everyone anticipated his mama's response. She did not disappoint. She poked her finger in his chubby little belly and said, "Uh-oh, *you*, mister." She then hugged him closely and began to laugh out loud. The tension immediately disappeared, and everyone let out the breath we'd collectively been holding. We all laughed until tears streamed down our faces. We handed the young mom Kleenex and handkerchiefs and called for a flight attendant to come rescue her and her precious baby.

I took my seat and, following some good conversation with my seatmates, settled in and began thinking about the moment. A question quickly came to mind. Let me ask you that same question. How many times, when you least expected it, has your world spewed all over you? How did you react? Were you able to gather yourself and choose to trust God, or did you find yourself covered in doubt, despair, and hopelessness?

The gentle reminder that day helped prepare me for difficult circumstances that were just ahead in my life. I did not know it right then, but as I strived to give Him control of my life, I believe God was preparing me for another battle. God knows my path and His plans for me and is always working in my life. I would often recall that moment with a smile on my face as I remembered how that mom had handled the mess with such grace. This story is a great reminder to ask God to give me a fresh new focus each day.

It shouldn't matter what unexpected or messy circumstances threaten our daily peace. Our choice should already have been made to stand firm and honor God. When life says, "Take that!" instead of freaking out, our response should be, "You've got this, Lord!"

Chapter 11

LOST AND ON ASSIGNMENT

❧

> *Do not be anxious about anything, but in*
> *every situation, by prayer and petition, with*
> *thanksgiving, present your requests to God.*
> *And the peace of God, which transcends all*
> *understanding, will guard your hearts and*
> *your minds in Christ Jesus.*
>
> Philippians 4:6–7

A s I've mentioned, airports are not for sissies. Jeff and I were in Phoenix, Arizona, for a meeting with some churches. After returning our rental car, we caught the shuttle to the terminal for the flight home. We were behind schedule and hurried to gather our bags and get inside.

When we stepped up to the counter to check in, I realized I had left my wallet with my ID in the rental car. Jeff proceeded to check in while I raced outside looking for the quickest *return* to the rental facility. I caught a break and jumped into the closest taxi, quickly explained my dilemma to the driver, and I was on my way. Her name was Wendy, and she was determined to get me back to my flight on time. We immediately connected as I told her the reason for my visit to Phoenix. She shared with me about a situation she was experiencing, and as she spoke, I realized I was in the middle of a "God Moment," or as my friend Teresa says, "I was on assignment."

I gave little thought to Jeff, who was back at the terminal in a mild state of panic. He had no idea how I would get on that plane if I did not find my ID. I didn't know if he would get on the plane and leave me to find my way home, or if he would stay and save me from myself. Of course, this would not be the first time I'd put him in a stressful situation. He knew it would be a story, but at that moment was not thrilled to be part of it.

Wendy got me to the rental facility, and I raced into the building while she waited for me. I went right to where we returned the car and began telling them what I'd done. They said the car had not been moved and I was free to go search through it. I ran to the car, opened the door, reached under the seat, and felt my wallet. Oh, the relief that flooded through me. With no time to waste, I yelled, "I found it! Thank you so much. Have a great day!" and began running back to my waiting ride. As Wendy spotted me, I waved my wallet and watched her shake her head with laughter.

I jumped in and we sped off back to the terminal. I opened my wallet to see if everything was in place and as I did, Wendy said, "Deb, would you pray for me? I'm short on money and have no food in the house. Pray God gives me some good rides today to meet my needs." I asked her directly how short she was, and she said, "I need another $100 by the end of the day so I can get some food for my kids and me and pay one bill." I looked down and my eyes fell on a $100 bill, which just happened to be lying there in my wallet. Immediately, I wondered, "Had I left my wallet so Wendy could feed her kids?" I knew that I was the resource God had chosen to help her. What a blessing to be used by God in His plan for this lady.

When Wendy pulled up to the terminal to drop me off, I paid her and then after a big hug, I handed her the bill. Her eyes filled with tears and she embraced me again, while telling me, "Run, Deb! Run!"

As I entered the terminal, the first person I saw was Jeff. He had stayed right where I'd left him to wait for my return. I was very emotional and, of course, out of breath. Jeff thought it was because I'd lost my wallet, but as I shared the story, he quickly realized we'd been part of a divine intervention. We made it through security and to the gate just as our boarding group was announced. We had a good laugh and gave God praise for showing us once again that He never wastes a moment of our lives.

Has the enemy of your soul robbed you of your "wallet" a time or two and caused you to walk in fear? God desires to use you. If you don't stay alert, you can easily wind up back on the porch, overwhelmed by circumstances, and miss the incredible assignments He has just for you. God chose you and me to be His hands and feet. We cannot allow ourselves to get caught up in the "what-ifs" of our lives.

> *Who comforts us in all our troubles, so that*
> *we can comfort those in any trouble with*

the comfort we ourselves receive from God
(2 Cor. 1:4).

Remember to look up and refocus. Live each day in expectation of miracles and opportunities designed for you alone. Practice living in abundance and freedom with every choice you make.

Chapter 12

FAITH EXPLOSION – SRI LANKA

THE PRAYER OF FAITH

Is anyone among you in trouble? Let them pray. Is anyone happy? Let them sing songs of praise. Is anyone among you **sick**? Let them call the elders of the church to pray over them and anoint them with oil in the name of the Lord. And the prayer offered in faith will make the sick person well; the Lord will raise them up. If they have sinned, they will be forgiven. Therefore, confess your sins to each other and pray for each other so that you may be healed. *The prayer of a righteous person is powerful and effective.*

James 5:13–16

If I were to ask you to think of a person that you know, or have known, who has exhibited great faith, who would come to your mind? I instantly think of my Grandma Taylor. I trace my Christian heritage to her, knowing she prayed faithfully for me throughout my life until she went home to be in the presence of Jesus. I knew her as a real-life prayer warrior. I distinctly remember the two evenly spaced worn holes in the small throw rug beside her rocking chair where she would kneel to pray. She had so much faith, and she never seemed to waver regardless of her circumstances. Grandma inspired me. I believed I was strong in my faith, until I received a telephone call early one Tuesday morning from Sri Lanka in 2009.

I was sitting at my desk in my office, putting the finishing touches on a regional training conference for Upward Sports when my phone rang. I picked it up and quickly suspected one of my friends was trying to prank me. The person on the other end wanted to know if I had a current passport and if I would come to Sri Lanka for a women's conference and be a keynote speaker.

I responded, "Sure. When do you want me to come, and *where* is Sri Lanka?" I sarcastically suggested. "I could come tomorrow." The voice on the line answered, "No. If you can come Sunday, that will work." I laughed and suddenly sensed something was not quite right.

An awkward pause followed as I slowly processed what I'd just heard, and then I asked, "Can we start over? And can you explain exactly who you are and what this call is about? I actually thought this was a joke."

"This is no joke. We want you to be our keynote speaker."

Evidently, through a friend of a friend, my name had been suggested as a possible speaker at an annual Women's

Aglow Conference. The catch was the event started the following Wednesday. There would be over two thousand women in attendance. The main speaker was an evangelist by the name of Shekhar. The other keynote speaker had just canceled because her visa had been denied.

The woman on the phone asked if I also knew anyone who could lead music for the worship services, since their music leader had also canceled last minute. I knew my husband would *not* fit in at a women's conference, so my sister-in-law, Jennifer, immediately came to mind. I told her I would do some checking and let her know by the next day. After getting answers to my many questions, I hung up with the understanding that she would check on flights and I would check with my husband. I also would pray overnight about my decision to go.

I got off the phone and began immediately doing research on Sri Lanka and realized it was *only* 8,473 miles from home. My research indicated that it is a small, independent nation that lies off the southern tip of India and had endured a long and bitter civil war. Sri Lanka is part of South Asia and, despite war, attracts many visitors because of its natural beauty. I also found out that it housed "sweatshops" that produced clothing for some of the biggest brand names, such as GAP, Victoria's Secret, Nike, Tommy Hilfiger, Ralph Lauren, and many others. Many websites suggested it was *not* safe to travel there.

Years before, when I began speaking at various functions and events, I had promised the Lord I would go wherever and whenever He provided unless I was sick or could not get time off work. My job with Upward was all about outreach, and I knew my supervisor would approve my going. Jeff had always been supportive of me and my speaking opportunities. As I prayed for God's direction, my answer became clear, and I began to watch God work out every detail as only He can do.

I called Jennifer and told her I had been invited to Sri Lanka and wanted her to go with me. Then I told her we would leave in *four* days and be gone for a week. I was ready with several reasons why I thought she needed to say yes, but to my shock and delight she was open to the idea and immediately peppered me with many questions.

The following day, Merina called me from Sri Lanka to tell me they could get us tickets for $4,000. I immediately felt checked and told her we could not allow them to pay that amount. She quickly replied, "No worries. It is just one or two dollars per person. We can cover it *easily* if you'll come?" I simply said, "Book it."

Although I had been public speaking for years, never had I spoken in a country slightly above third-world status, and I had *no* idea how I would deal with the language barrier. I began to pray about what to share and how to connect with the ladies and immediately had some clear insight. I have always believed that if the gospel is preached with truth, it can go anywhere to any people. My belief was about to be tested yet again, more than I ever imagined.

We left on Sunday from Spokane, Washington, and arrived Tuesday night in Sri Lanka. The flight was to be extremely long, so we were thrilled when both of us were upgraded to business class from Denver to London.

The conference began on Wednesday morning, and my first speaking engagement was Wednesday afternoon. I was inspired and excited to share what I felt God had given me, even though I suffered slightly from jet lag. I had been speaking to the conference attendees for forty-five minutes when I noticed a subtle hand motion from Sylvia, our director, signaling me to keep going. On the spot, I began to share more stories and quote more scripture. Thirty minutes later, I got the nod that I could close. Whew! What a beginning. It was so unlike America, where attention spans are closer to twenty minutes, wristwatch and phone alarms are set, and if you do speak longer, you better have good reason.

The following day, I was the first speaker in the afternoon session. I felt inspired as I preached to these incredible women. After I finished and returned to my seat, Shekhar came forward and closed the afternoon session with a healing service. I watched in amazement as literally hundreds of women lined up for healing. The needs were *so* great. My heart was touched as people's lives were changed.

As I was watching and taking it all in, my mind was swirling with so many emotions. I was apprehensive while at the same time in awe of what God was doing. There was no doubt that I was experiencing a holy moment. My heart was pounding, and I could not close my eyes because I didn't want to miss any part of this experience.

Suddenly, Shekhar motioned for me to move forward and help by laying on hands and praying with ladies. Yikes! I was caught off-guard and not prepared for this. I know, I know ... practice what you preach ... right?

I had come to Sri Lanka on faith and knew God was using me, but I'd never felt like God had called me or anointed me with the gift of healing. As I stood and took my place, trembling and full of unease, a line quickly formed with those who needed prayer. What happened next was humbling, humiliating, and life changing.

The very first person was a small, elderly lady dressed in a beautiful sari. She stood humbly before me, hands clasped and her face beaming with hope. As she looked up at me, I saw her eyes were covered with what I assumed were cataracts. She asked me to pray that God would remove the cataracts. I immediately became excited and thought I could relate to her. I said to her, "Oh sweet friend, my mom had cataracts and just had surgery. She can see perfectly now, even better than before, and does not even need glasses. You can have surgery and be as good as new."

I know what you are thinking, right? Honestly, I was sharing my heart and was humbled to my core when this sweet little lady put both hands on my face, looked directly at me and said, "No, I have nooooooo money. I have *never* seen a doctor. You must *pray* that God heals me so I can take care of my family. God sent you here to pray for me."

Oh dear, now what?

I dug deep for every ounce of faith I had and told this dear woman that although I did not have the gift of healing, I personally knew the Healer and believed that He would touch her, and I began to pray. I wept and I prayed, and I laid hands on this child of God and finally said my amen. There was no visible instant healing. We embraced, and with God's blessing I sent her on her way.

This woman had nothing according to our American standards. She was dressed in the only sari she owned. She was nothing but a servant to her husband, and she told me she had been saving money for two years to be able to come to the conference.

When we got back to our room, I was devastated. How could I be so shallow and how could my faith be so weak? This woman believed 100 percent that God could heal her and that He would do it through *my* prayers. I fought to resist my doubt all night and into the next morning. I got out of bed praying that I could find words to inspire and motivate these amazing Sri Lankan women to stay the course and receive their redemption. I felt unworthy and inadequate for the task ahead that day. I remember sitting quietly at breakfast, asking God to use me—even through my weaknesses. I surrendered my smallness and asked Him to open heaven for these wonderful, God-fearing women.

When I got to the meeting room that morning, there was a buzz. I do not know how else to describe it. Usually at conferences, when we arrive in the morning it is to a quiet setting with small groups visiting in hushed conversations. But today? Today was noticeably different. There was an excitement that seemed to snap and crackle like electricity in the air. And then it happened.

We were slowly making our way down the aisle when the sea of ladies parted, and my little saint walked up to me and exclaimed, "Debbieeeee, look!" What I saw were two remarkably clear eyes looking straight through to my soul. I could not speak. I could hardly breathe as I took in the sight. I hugged her and together we praised God for touching her. She softly reached up and touched my cheek and said, "I told you God would use you. Next time, your faith will be stronger. You and God have work to do."

My faith needed to be challenged because I had fallen into the trap of trusting knowledge more than God, circumstances more than God, even friends and family more than God. When did I begin to think of God as my second or third choice? I do not remember her name and can barely remember her face, but I will *always* remember her words to me that morning.

> *And my God will meet all your needs*
> *according to the riches of his glory in Christ*
> *Jesus* (Phil. 4:19).

That verse now has deep meaning, and when I quote it or say it out loud, I am reminded that with God, all things are possible. When He takes my tiny faith and adds His supernatural power, I will proclaim, "Nothing Is Impossible!"

> *Is anyone among you sick? Let them call the*
> *elders of the church to pray over them and*
> *anoint them with oil in the name of the Lord.*
> *And the prayer offered in faith will make the*
> *sick person well; the Lord will raise them*
> *up. If they have sinned, they will be forgiven*
> (Jms. 5:14–15).

The miracle of this story is that I thought I was going to Sri Lanka to bring the Word to thousands of women. God knew that Deb Weisen needed to be shaken to the core if she was to continue being used for His glory. Since that day, I have had many opportunities to pray for healing. I always begin those prayers by reminding all who are present, including myself, to whom we are speaking and who has the power to heal. Once we get centered on the King who is our Jehovah Jireh (the Lord will provide) and Jehovah Rapha (the Lord who heals you), we can then pray in faith with deep conviction and steadfast belief and trust.

I told you about my grandma, but did I mention that she also had very little? Yet she was the richest woman I have ever known because she found all her needs met in Christ alone. No grand house, no immaculate, landscaped yard. Just a simple orchard, a cow to milk, a few chickens for eggs, and a family that adored and honored her. She was rich. When we all had homemade ice cream at Grandma's, we knew it was because God had somehow blessed her with some extra money to buy sugar. Whenever she was blessed, we were blessed.

God expanded my faith much deeper and wider that week in Sri Lanka because I obeyed Him. He wants to do the same for you. Are you ready? When was the last time you stepped out in faith and allowed God to transform you and mold you? I challenge you right now to stop walking in apathy and safety and dive head-first into unexplainable, undeniable, supernatural living. It's quite remarkable!

Chapter 13

A LOVE LETTER REWRITTEN

*You will not have to fight this battle. Take up your **positions**; stand **firm** and **see** the **deliverance** the LORD will give you, Judah and Jerusalem. Do not be afraid; do not be discouraged. Go out to face them tomorrow, and the LORD will be with you.*

2 Chronicles 20:17

I love my Bible. It has had three new covers now, and my life story and many of the stories of my children are detailed in its well-worn pages. Dates that have great meaning to me are recorded there. February 1, 1975 is recorded as the day I made my personal, *total* commitment to Jesus Christ. I've looked at that date many times and been moved to tears. Forty-six years later, I know without a doubt that moment changed my life forever and changed the course I would take in the years that followed.

Through much effort, I have memorized chapters, verses, and even books of the Bible. I can see the words on the pages because I am so familiar with this Bible. I tell you this because I know for sure that the only way to stand firm, walk in thanksgiving and joy, and be surrounded by peace is to stay in God's Word. There have been very few times in my life where I have set my Bible on a stand and not opened it every day. When I have needed a reminder, God has always been faithful to remind me that this book is a gift to me, a love letter that I can open every morning. As we come to the end of this part of my journey, I have one more story to share. It is one of the most inspirational God-Moments in my life.

Life has a way of crowding out even our most sincere efforts if we do not remain alert to the Spirit and His still, small voice. In retrospect, somehow my daily quiet time had become a routine. God reminded me that I had become very passive with my Bible and had been taking it for granted.

It was Friday morning in Sri Lanka, and I was extremely excited about what I was going to share that afternoon. I was sitting in the conference, listening to Shekhar preach when I began to sense a different message forming in my heart and mind. I had been taking notes, so I quickly began to jot down an outline as it came to me. In all my years of teaching and preaching, I had *never* written a message in twenty minutes. As I sat there, I knew God was directing my thoughts. At lunch I asked Jennifer, my sister-in-law, to pray, and I told her about the message. It would go hand in hand with my life scripture found in 2 Chronicles 20.

In this story, King Jehoshaphat is being invaded by armies from Ammon, Moab, and Mount Seir. He declares that he does not know what to do, but his eyes are upon God. After much prayer, the Spirit of the Lord came upon Jahaziel and he stood in the assembly and said,

> *"Listen, King Jehoshaphat, and all who live in Judah and Jerusalem! This is what the LORD says to you: "Do not be afraid or discouraged because of this vast army. FOR THE BATTLE IS NOT YOURS BUT GOD'S. Tomorrow march down against them. They will be climbing up by the Pass of Ziz, and you will find them at the end of the gorge in the Desert of Jeruel. You will not have to fight this battle. **Take up your positions; stand firm** and **see** the **deliverance** the LORD will give you, O Judah and Jerusalem."*

Those three commands are so clear: (1) Take up your position, (2) Stand firm, and (3) Wait for God's deliverance.

Too often we are not prepared and in position when we find ourselves in the middle of a battle. When we finally realize our predicament, it can be extremely difficult to overcome the enemy. We *must* choose first who we will serve and who we will trust so when the battle does come, we can *stand firm*, always remembering we never have to stand alone.

It is like teenagers committing to stay pure *before* they begin dating. We know that once they start dating, they will struggle to stand firm if their decision hasn't been cemented. The pressure to compromise their purity can be overwhelming.

When we take up our position *and* we are standing firm, we can then wait confidently for God's deliverance. I know, we all hate that four-letter word ... *wait*. God's deliverance always comes—it's just not always the way we expect it and it's not necessarily on our time schedule.

All these thoughts were in my mind as we approached the afternoon session where I was to speak. Jennifer led music and did a wonderful job setting the tone for the acceptance of the Word I was about to share. I'd been preaching for about twenty minutes when I began to unveil the best weapon I used to stand firm in the face of any battle with the enemy—*memorizing* and *quoting* scripture. It is, after all, the sword included with the armor of God. I held up my Bible and said, "This Bible must become your weapon against the enemy. You must read it and memorize it and know what God says about holy living. You'll find power in the *Word* of God." I was feeling inspired and preaching with passion. I felt I was on a roll, so to speak. Suddenly, a lady in the front row raised her hand and stopped me. I had never actually had anyone do that while I was speaking and was taken back by the interruption. I stopped, looked at her, and said, "Do you have a question?" She replied, "No. I have to tell *you* something, *Debbieeee*. We *do not* have Bibles. Even if we could afford them, we are not allowed by our husbands to have Bibles."

You've heard the phrase, "Take the wind right out of your sails..." or as a good friend of mine says, "That'll jam your preserves." I stood there thinking, "Help me, Lord! What am I to do and *why* did You lead me down this path?" After what seemed like several minutes, I said, "Oh dear, I do not know what to say to that. But *this*, I do know. I serve the Creator of the universe, and He alone has a creative solution to every problem so I cannot wait to see how He plans to answer this need." *That's* what came to me at that moment. I smiled weakly and then continued my sermon.

Following the service, I went to my room wondering how I could have been so clueless. It seemed like everything on which I had based my life was in question. The women were responding, but I was left feeling as though, in some way, I had not spoken what God had wanted the women to hear. I kept asking Him if I'd missed something and begged Him to use my words for *His* glory despite the difficult dilemma these women faced.

Saturday morning arrived after a long night of reflection, and I was determined to finish strong. Shekhar had flown home to India the day before, so I was the only speaker on the schedule for this final morning of the conference. Jennifer and I headed to breakfast, and I noticed that there were no napkins at the table. When I requested one, our waitress said, "I'm so sorry, but we are temporarily out of all paper goods." Well, that was unusual, and even odd, I thought, but I gently said, "Oh well, that's okay. No worries. Thank you."

When we walked into the service, the room was again filled with the same electricity we had experienced just a few days before. Small groups of women were sharing together. Shortly after, we found out why the hotel was out of all paper goods. A group of about twenty to thirty women had stayed up the *entire* night and had *handwritten* scriptures on toilet paper, napkins, and any scrap piece of paper they could find anywhere in the hotel. They told us that God had inspired them to write down as many scriptures as they could so they could share them with each other and then pass them from household to household. I saw chapter after chapter of scripture. They also informed us that because the papers were small, they could easily be hidden in their homes. They would each take a portion, memorize it, and then pass it on to the next home and wait to receive another piece of paper containing another portion of God's holy Word.

I was in complete awe of what God had inspired.

The women were exhausted, yet their joy and excitement were contagious. They shared how they were creating a battle plan to help each other stand firm.

In my mind, I could see my bookshelves at home that were lined with Bibles of every version. *I realized that I had allowed my abundance to plague my spiritual health*—again, a reminder that I had begun to trust everything but God because I had so much. As Jennifer led music that morning before I closed with my final sermon, I stood for the singing, but my spirit was bowed low in humble gratitude to my God who *never* fails. The words of a song rang through my soul, "I stand, I stand in awe of you!" The only God, the Creator of the universe, had reminded me that His ways are definitely *not* my ways. He is so much bigger than my small mind can even imagine. This was a powerful reminder to me that I must take up my position and stand firm by totally trusting God in all my circumstances. This is the only way I will find joy and real peace in waiting for Him to deliver me.

My foundations were cemented by a trip to Sri Lanka that would forever stay in my memory as my own personal revival. God took me 8,473 miles to a group of loving, caring, extraordinary women to get my attention and renew my faith. But let me end my story with this—we do *not* have to travel halfway around the world to have our faith renewed in a fresh, new way. God wants to revive us today, right where we are.

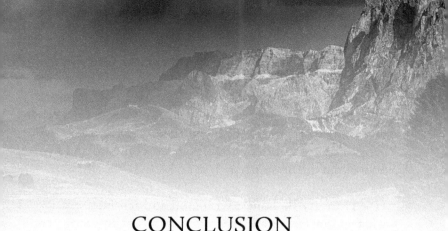

CONCLUSION

W hat a God we serve! If we walk in obedience, He will do whatever it takes to enable us to stand firm and live expectantly as we wait for His final deliverance. At times we are tempted to trust the lies of the giants in our lives. They seem powerful and unbeatable, yet just like David, we must *not* give them a second thought. Our response should resound loud and clear just as the Scripture declares, "You come against me with sword and spear and javelin, but I come against you in the name of the LORD Almighty!" (1 Sam. 17:45)

Whatever the giants we may face—fear, uncertainty, rejection, failure, or the sense of being out of control—they remain *powerless* when we come against them in the name of the Lord God Almighty. Our entire focus must remain on God. He is the One we are to magnify and glorify. When we glorify Him, His light reveals how fallible the giants really are. God will render them powerless when we refuse to trust anything or anyone other than Him. God alone is our hope and power.

What this world really needs right now is *hope*. Hope is, by definition, a feeling of expectation and desire for a certain thing to happen, a feeling of trust. Use the following acrostic as you continue to fix your eyes on God and live above your circumstances.

H – Honesty Be honest with God and tell Him exactly what you are feeling and where you are struggling. Stop performing and pretending and begin to openly tell God about your fear, shame, and guilt.

O – Optimism Expect the best possible outcome. Stop dwelling on the what-ifs and the oh-no's and live expecting God to work on your behalf. Remember that no matter what you are facing, the Creator of the universe has a creative solution to *every* problem. Live with expectation and optimism.

P – Prayer Pray as if your life depends on it, because it does! Praying continually will strengthen your relationship with the King of Kings. Stay in conversation with God throughout the day, asking for His help to be honest and optimistic in your faith.

E – Effort It takes effort to walk in step with the Spirit. We must trust the Holy Spirit for His guidance. In doing so, we can discern His path to living a holy and abundant life. The Spirit is faithful to remind us when our choices lead us to doubt or waiver.

> *Therefore, with minds that are alert and fully sober, **set** your hope on the grace to be*

*brought to you when Jesus Christ is revealed
at his coming.* **1 Peter 1:13**

Make a conscious choice to set your hope, your heart, *and* your mind on Jesus Christ. Live expectantly and overcome the giants in your life by seeking a fresh view from the porch.

CPSIA information can be obtained
at www.ICGtesting.com
Printed in the USA
BVHW052235280621
610637BV00004B/776